MOSAICS

D1529530

Contents

Chapter 2

MATERIALS AND TOOLS

Chapter 1

THE MOSAIC

chapter
TECHNIQUES

chapter
PROJECTS

Introduction

A mosaic can be ideal for decorating any object or environment, because it combines traditional techniques with creative solutions. The use of new materials with novel approaches lets us create mosaics on any surface and for all environments. While overcoming the traditional limits, mosaics are rooted in an expressive discipline of the first order. In this book we offer a wide, vigorous, and didactic look at the innumerable possibilities for this art as a decorative technique. First, the theoretic fundamentals are explained from a technical and historical point of view, as well as the attributes that this artistic medium is based on, the qualities of the mosaic, and its limitless possibilities.

Next, after the chapter on materials and tools, the techniques are explained in full detail. Special effort has been made to show the basic technical processes at all stages of the work, explaining them fully through practical examples, and emphasizing the ones that best lend themselves to creative freedom. The step-by-step projects illustrate the complete processes of ten interior and exterior decorative approaches. These practical projects were completed to inspire anyone who wishes to learn and make progress in this art. They encompass solutions, techniques, and ideas that suggest approaches that can be applied to everyone's needs, and that will help them establish their own creative path.

Philippa Beveridge and Eva Pascual

chapter

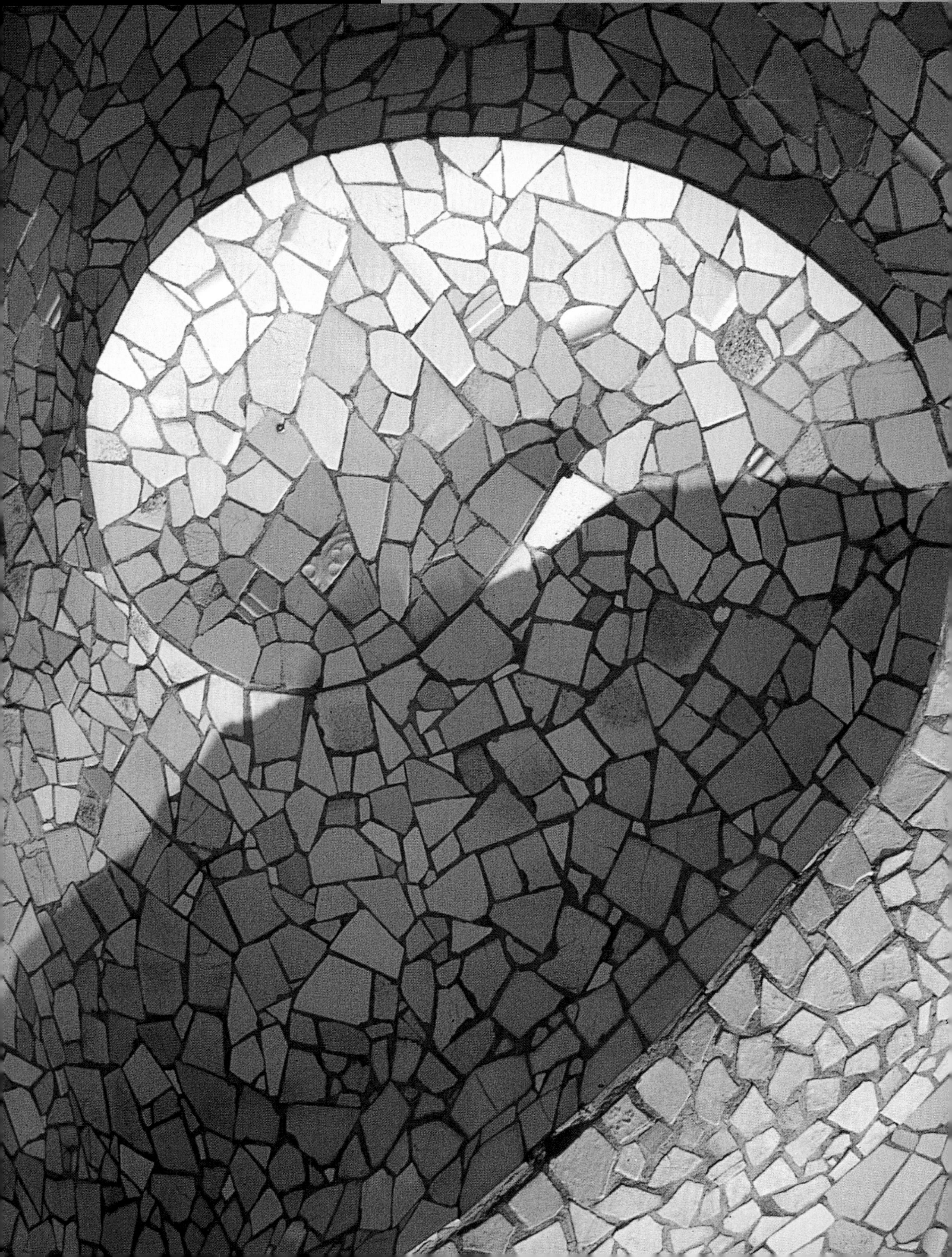

1

The Mosaic

The mosaic medium offers a wonderful way to
approach the world of decorative arts. An artistic
discipline with its own unique language, it allows
very personal work where the limits are one's own
creativity. The work done in mosaic can be
adapted to any style and become fully integrated
into the decoration, adding to it its own unique
attributes. Artistically, it is capable of very
complex results, although there are options for
all levels of skill. Mastery is achieved through
the constant practice of its language and
technique, and the knowledge of its history.

The Art of Mosaic

The word mosaic derives from the Latin term *Musa*, which described the mural decorations of the grottoes in Roman gardens dedicated to the muses.

This is an ancient art; the first known examples date back to prehistoric times, and they still survive today. It has experienced an important resurgence, a new appreciation that considers it to be a very highly expressive artistic medium.

Technique

Until the end of the nineteenth century and beginning of the twentieth, mosaic has been considered a parallel discipline to painting; it was able to create pictures that were more durable than paintings. Direct techniques were employed by the artisans of the Greek and Roman Eras and during the Byzantine and Medieval Periods. They worked equally on floors and walls, placing the tiles according to the locations marked in the sketch or drawing (traced from a previously made design) onto the mortar or prepared surface. The tiles were embedded directly onto the top layer of mortar while it was still fresh. Later it was grouted with a mixture of marble, sand, and lime, as in the Roman Era.

In Venice, in the thirteenth century, mosaics used the tradition of painting *al fresco* as a sort of sketch. The paint applied to the freshly prepared wall served as a guide to the placement of the tiles, and the color of the seams reinforced the chromatic attributes of the mosaic; the gaps were an integral part of the work.

Detail of *The Traveling Musicians,* a mosaic by Dioscurides of Samos, copy of a composition from the second or first century B.C.

During the Roman Period mosaics were also created on separate supports (*emblemata*) and later inset into a final location. It is believed that during the Byzantine Period some figures were created separately and inset into mosaics from the back, but the technique that was used then is not known. It wasn't until the Modernist Period, between the nineteenth and twentieth centuries, that mosaic techniques were revolutionized, production was industrialized, and solutions were found as quickly as new needs arose.

Chimneys of the Palacio Güell in Barcelona, Spain, designed by Antoni Gaudí, 1886–1891.

Detail of the right side of the *mihrab* in the Gran Mezquita of Córdoba, tenth century.

Origins and Some Historic Dates

The oldest examples of mosaic date to the prehistoric era in Neolithic Crete and to Greece in the late Bronze Age (about 1600–1000 B.C.). They are pavers made with small stones that were embedded in the mortar on the ground. During the Greek era this art was perfected with the introduction of colored stones, which demonstrates interest in creating picture effects. Tiles of stone and glass came into common use during the Hellenistic Period. But the great advances in mosaic came during the Roman Empire. The floors, walls, and niches were decorated with mosaics in full-color, naturalistic representations dominated by pictorial components. Each placement system used (*opus*) received a particular denomination—those of the walls were distinguished from those of the floors, and the artisans that made them also were called by different names. Gen-

erally, stone materials were used for the floors and vitreous paste (enamels) were used for mosaics on the walls. Some mosaics were portable, and in addition to their function as architectural coverings, could be used as pictures.

The art of Roman mosaic began to decline during the fourth century A.D., during the rule of the Byzantine Empire. During the entire era, with a peak period during the fourth to the seventh centuries, but lasting until the thirteenth century, important mosaic works were created that supplanted painting. These works, limited to the walls of cult sites, have a strong courtly component where the naturalism of the previous era was replaced by stately looking figures. During the Medieval Period in Europe the use of mosaics was limited to floors; later, during the Renaissance and until the nineteenth century, they were used for making works that are equivalent to paintings, but more lasting. It was the arrival of Modernism that reestablished the importance of this art and set the stage for its later development.

Façade of the old Casa Figueras building, now a pastry shop, in Barcelona, designed by Antoni Ros i Güell, 1902.

Tendencies

It is obvious that today there is interest in mosaic and its great decorative potential. Since the mid-1980s there has been a spectacular resurgence of mosaic, which has become a valid approach for decorating any environment. Now the unique properties of the work are highly valued, the pieces made to order for a location where they will fit into a creative and singular decor, in contrast to stereotyped decoration done with mass-produced objects. To that can be added the growing importance of craft, which is valuable in itself (as opposed to what happened at the beginning of the twentieth century), and the commercial value that our society gives arts and crafts. At the same time, mosaic achieves the difficult conjunction of esthetics and practicality, creating, depending on the case and the materials, very durable surfaces. Today, new technical and formal areas are being explored, looking at mosaic as an artistic medium. Technically speaking, it is enough to point out the infinite possibilities offered by the use of computers related to creating designs, as well as cutting and placing the pieces. Notable examples of avant-garde architecture have made use of them. One example is the wall covering of the Santa Catalina market in Barcelona, work of the architectural studio of E. Miralles and B. Tagliabue, covered with ceramic pieces in mosaic form, the construction of which was to be finished in 2004. Regarding the formal possibilities, these go hand-in-hand with the use of new materials such as linoleum (so far we are only aware of examples by Damien Morrison), and wood, and other organic coverings such as coconut husk that have been properly treated.

Mosaics can be integrated in any setting, becoming part of the design itself. Philippa Beveridge, 1993.

Decoration of a domed roof in Can Roca, in Esparraguera, Barcelona. Lívia Garreta, 1989. Photograph by Toni Coll.

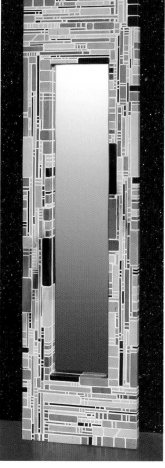

Mirror with a frame made of pieces of linoleum. Damien Morrison, 2002.

Sources of Inspiration

Sources of inspiration are valuable to the creative process required for the creation of any work. They become the ideal medium for stimulating creativity, offering ideas, effects, and approaches that, when reinterpreted constitute the work of art.

When speaking of making mosaics these sources are unlimited; our surroundings offer us limitless approaches that can be used as a departure point for making mosaics.

Objects

Common objects can become motifs that are developed into a figurative or abstract design, to become a pattern for a mosaic work. Anything can be a departure point for designing a mosaic, whether they are objects of daily use, or machines, pieces, fabrics, etc. In this sense, printed fabrics offer many sources of inspiration. The motifs and colors of the fabric can be the key to elaborating decorative fabrics based on the repetition or combination of patterns extracted and interpreted from the original.

Any objects, in this case, gear wheels, can serve as inspirations for creativity.

Nature

A butterfly posed on a flower offers a very decorative image.

Nature offers us numerous resources for making mosaics, whether through direct observation or using images. The plant world represents a vast array of forms and colors from which to extract motifs. Plants offer limitless ideas that can be applied to mosaics, whether they are complete and become the central theme, or using one element to create a background or border, for example. In this sense, the important esthetic component of flowers causes them to be one of the most commonly used motifs. Fruit and vegetables are also common themes. The animal kingdom also presents a wide variety of creative motifs, from mollusks and fish to domestic animals. Like landscapes, they can be natural or transformed by human action.

Historic Mosaics

Copying and reinterpreting original mosaics is an excellent point of departure for creating work. The possibilities are not limited to literal copies but can be amplified by using elements taken from scenes (people, animals, or plants, borders) as central motifs of the work you wish to create.

The border design taken from a Roman mosaic serves as a motif for a mosaic.

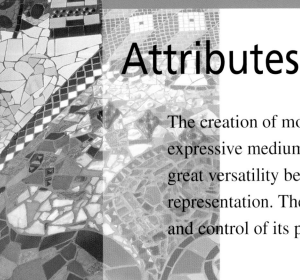

Attributes

The creation of mosaic works is based on understanding the expressive medium through its unique techniques. This art allows great versatility because it can be used in making any representation. The success of the final result depends on the use and control of its potential in the interpretation.

The Attributes of Mosaics

Traditionally, the language of mosaics, when speaking of the artistic discipline, has developed parallel to that of painting. The art has historically been expressed with a language similar to that of painting, feeling the effects of the limitations of a medium that tries to imitate another, although they share some aspects when it comes to representing two dimensions. Nevertheless, mosaic is not limited to two-dimensional representation; it can also be used to create three-dimensional works. It is, therefore, an artistic discipline with its own attributes that often differ from those that are strictly related to painting, and it should be understood in that way. The qualities of a mosaic, its attributes, (design, color, placement, contrast, and texture, among others), are essential components that must be taken into account when creating the work, since knowledge of them is the basis upon which the language rests. It is also important to dominate the artistic medium and control the solutions that you wish to achieve.

This decorative panel is on the façade of a pharmacy in Barcelona. Color is the predominant value of this mosaic. The central motif (the plant) is made from areas of color, which vividly contrast with the white background, and the undulating lines of the stems and leaves add movement to the composition.

Design

Four basic components play a role in the design of any composition: form, line, shape, and color. Form refers to the figure of the object that you wish to represent; if it is a three-dimensional object and you wish to show its volume, this can be done using gradations of colors and tones and using shading. Line is used for marking and defining the edges of the work, as well as for representing its parts and elements. Shape refers to the silhouette, and color refers to the chromatic attributes of the scene. Making a mosaic requires a preliminary design, and the assembly requires the elaboration of a final sketch. It contains the attributes that you wish to transmit, emphasizing the component or components that inspired the selection and creation of the representation, or focusing on those with which you wish to work. The choices are based on esthetic criteria. However, some components or factors that are specific to the technique will affect the results of the final work and should be considered. The lines and spaces between the pieces are part of the work; they are crucial in defining the results; they determine the final effect, and sometimes they are more noticeable than any other visual aspect. The placement of the pieces, or tiles, that is to say, the model or pattern for arranging them, defines both the design and the execution of the work, so the placement (type, spacing between pieces, color) and arrangement become components of the design.

This mosaic is based on the central scene, which is completed with a combination of forms and colors. The umbrella, in black and white, contrasting with the blue background, is made with larger pieces than the blue, and is cut and arranged to suggest the volumes of the fabric. The fruit at the bottom is made with rounded pieces that contrast with the rectangular forms of the background. *Memory of Home*, Ellen Stern.

This mosaic, based on a model with a linear style, was made by combining pieces and colors that emphasize this component.

Color

Color is one of the aspects with great and interesting potential in the creation of mosaics. Color is the sensation produced in the eye of the viewer by the light reflected from a surface in a determined band of the spectrum. Color depends on how we capture the light that is reflected by the surfaces in our surroundings, and therefore it influences our perception of the world.

Colors and Sensations

Colors transmit sensations and influence people's physical and psychological states, inducing sensations of irritation, tension, pleasure, relaxation, spirituality, and passion, among others. It is thought that the preference or dislike for specific colors or color combinations, as well as some feelings such as satisfaction, difficulty, security, and excitation, are associated with personal psychological components and experiences, even from very early stages in life. Psychological and philosophical components are associated with colors, varying from one person to another, and depending on the environment and cultural traditions. The only universally accepted classification is based on the physical components of color: reds, oranges, and yellows are considered warm colors, while blues, greens, and violets are considered to be cold.

A group of the warm colors, the earth tones (ochers, siennas, oxides, moss greens, reddish browns, etc.) are instinctively associated with joy and

Decoration, achieved with ceramic pieces, which is based on contrasts obtained by combining colors.
Front of a commercial center in Roca del Vallès in Barcelona. Lívia Garreta, 1998.

Detail of front piece. The composition, an asymmetrically formed execution, is the result of wise combinations of cold and warm colors. The visual impact falls on the warm colors, located in the upper right area, which is the area where the eyes tend to focus. To balance the composition, orange pieces have been placed on the other side, that is, on the lower and upper left areas. The areas with cold colors also have been balanced.

cordiality; they symbolize profound and basic values, and while some people find them attractive, others perceive them as dull and uninteresting. Red is a provocative and passionate color; it attracts attention and is the center of interest, while bluish red and pink are considered sensual and voluptuous. Bright pink (magenta) is exciting, associated with fun and happiness, and brown is perceived as an elegant color. Generally, the yellows, oranges, and reds are happy and stimulating, although many people find them excessively provocative, and able to cause excitement.

Among the cool colors, green is tranquil and relaxing; it is associated with nature and open spaces, although some consider light green to be a boring color. The yellow-greens indicate nostalgia and melancholy. The grays communicate calm; they are considered to foment curiosity, reflection, and imagination, although nearly everyone finds them dull. Dark blue and the range of blue tones are associated with marine depths; they transmit a feeling of silence and calm, and they create the impression of depth; however, some blue tones suggest melancholy and loneliness.

During the creative process the choice of any color carries with it an implicit emotional message. The use of color and its limitless combinations always requires reflection based on experimentation so that in each case they support the message you wish to communicate.

A green tonal gradation made with squares.

A tonal gradation from white to blue based on a light gradation of middle-tone squares.

A tonal gradation from dark brown to white using gradations of middle-tone squares.

Tonal gradation from maroon to pink using squares.

Components of Color

Tone, intensity, and shade are also important components of color. By tone we understand the variation in a color through the addition of black or white, while the shade is the variation in a color due to the addition of another color. The intensity depends on the level of saturation of a color, that is, its qualities when it is in its purest state. Combining pieces of different tones and shades, and the creation of tonal gradations, opens up a wide range of formal possibilities when the mosaic reveals a language of pictorial components. Just as in painting, the intensity of color in a particular area or point in the work will affect the balance of the composition. The tonal transition must be made using combinations of pieces or tiles, either as a background of flat color, or as a light gradation of intermediate tones on the surface, transitioning the middle tones with the tiles in line or sequence from one tone to another without using intermediate tones. However, mosaics are more than just strictly pictorial compositions, since the combinations of pieces of different materials allow the creation of reflective and depth effects typical of this language.

Assembling the mosaic also becomes a basic component when it comes to the color. The tone of the grout used to fill the gaps between the pieces interferes

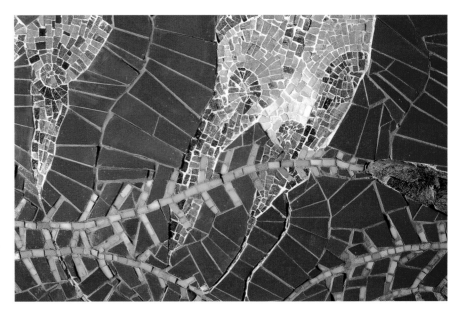

Here the contrast is defined by the colors (reds and blues), and emphasized by the grout and the combination of materials (glass tile and glazed tile) with different placement patterns.

with their colors, and this alters our perception of the chromatic combinations. Some artists believe that the color of the grout should be similar to the predominant tone of the mosaic. This way, mosaics made with light tones would be filled with white mortar or grout, mosaics that are mostly made with middle tones would use gray grout, and those with dark tones would use black. But other artists do not go by this, and even go against these guidelines to create effects and contrasts, emphasizing the specific colors of the pieces, creating contrasts between the background and the form, or unifying the look of the mosaic, for example. It is also possible

to not use grout, creating a mosaic based on the color effects of the pieces, although this would strictly limit the use of the work to interior decoration.

This mosaic was grouted with gray mortar to unify the light colors (white) and neutrals (light ocher and cream) with the dark ones (black and brown) and the orange. *Lilies,* Philippa Beveridge, 2004.

Contrast

Contrast, understood as comparison and opposition of the notable differences between two things, can be defined in various ways in mosaics. It is possible to create contrasts using color and tone, combining similar pieces of different materials, and in the pattern, that is, the placement and direction of the pieces and tiles. This can also be done through the combination of different materials to achieve contrasting effects based on characteristics such as surface and volume, and material qualities such as texture, sheen, shade, transparency, and opacity. But the most commonly used system for creating contrasts is based on the form and size of the pieces. The combination of different forms created by cutting (triangles and circles for making a flower, for example) and pieces of various sizes (the squares used to create a background, for example) all of the same material is a widely used approach.

You may think that all is valid when creating contrasts, but nothing is farther from the truth. Contrast is an element that attempts to transmit and form part of the interpretation of the mosaic, which is why it should be planned. Its success is based on the premise that opposites are complementary and they work when they are combined.

The sinuous form of the running bench is emphasized by the ceramic pieces. The multicolor backrest, made with many different tiles, contrasts with the white seat. Both parts relate to each other thanks to the circular white elements systematically arranged on the backrest. The circles contrast with the multicolor background. This is a view of the bench that surrounds the plaza at Parque Güell in Barcelona, work of Antoni Gaudí, 1900–1914.

Here is a detail of the bench. The contrast defines the form and color, the lower red piece stands out because of its circular shape on a background of broken, irregular, multicolor fragments with predominantly cool colors.

Broken ceramic pieces of different sizes were used to create a tonal contrast between the projecting and recessed parts of the chimney, thus emphasizing the volumes of the architecture. Detail of the roof of the Casa Milá, also known as La Pedrera, in Barcelona, work of Antoni Gaudí, 1906–1910.

Placement

A mosaic has specific components that affect the artistic aspects. The way that the pieces and tiles are arranged and placed on the surface to create a mosaic (called *andamenti*) is an essential part of this art and a primary element of the design and later execution of the work. The placement creates a series of lines between the pieces, defining their dimensions and forms. The lines, at the same time, emphasize the structure or pattern and define the rhythm of the composition. For example, straight lines will make more static compositions, while curved lines suggest movement and life.

Placement also is a fundamental tool of the design, since it allows the creation of multiple effects. Changes in the direction of the arrangement can be used to separate areas of the work or to relate areas of different colors. They can also indicate directionality, creating changes in the forms to highlight some chromatic effect. It is possible to combine different patterns in the same mosaic to create a form, separating it from the background of the composition through the different placements of the pieces, for example.

The pieces or tiles can be arranged in a great variety of patterns, involving other attributes such as design and color. It is possible to place them in grids, staggered, in a fan shape, in circles, or in wavy lines. Blocks or lines can be made to create changes of color, and color gradations made in horizontal lines. The rhythm and form of the outline of the main subject can be followed to emphasize it, and an outline can be made around it as well.

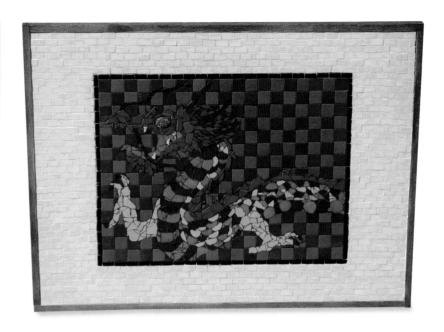

The central motif, a dragon of oriental inspiration, is framed by a green background made with tiles placed in a grid, the two tones alternating in a checkerboard pattern. The animal stands out from the background because of the arrangement and color. The head and the back are made with triangular and polygonal pieces whose many angles contrast with the grid-shaped background. The body was made with rounded pieces suggesting scales, accentuating the curve of the front part of the dragon. The eye, an oval piece with some volume, is the focal point. The colors of the body and the legs, which are warm colors, contrast with the blue-colored head and back (cool color) and the background. The black border and the white area that surround the motif also participate in the composition. *Dragon T*, Ellen Stern.

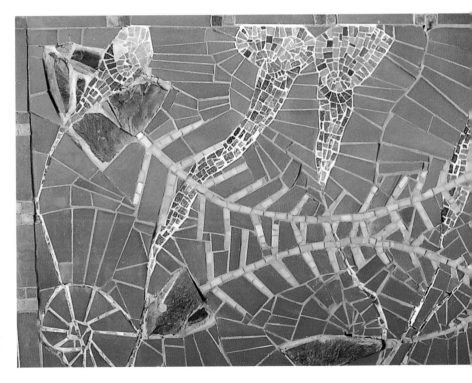

This mosaic combines the ceramic tile in the background cut in large fragments and arranged in a fan shape, with small pieces placed in different directions to configure the subjects. Philippa Beveridge, 1993.

Different kinds of placement are combined in this mosaic, creating an interesting play of forms. The square patterns placed to form wavy lines crossing over each other, the exterior outlining of the form, the fan arrangement of the central area, and the broken pieces in the background, along with the play of colors, volumes, and textures, are cleverly combined to form a very decorative surface. Detail of the roof in Can Roca, in Esparraguerra, Barcelona. Work by Lívia Garreta, 1989. Photograph by Toni Coll.

The placement and colors define the elements of this mosaic. The tree, made of tiles placed to indicate the verticality of the curving trunk, contrast with the background, which follows a pattern that emphasizes horizontality. Detail of an eighth-century mosaic in the Great Mosque of Damascus, Syria.

Placement is a defining tool in the composition. Here, the juxtaposition of two patterns of similar placement but in different directions defines the rhythm of the composition.

Texture

Texture, which is based on visual and tactile elements, is a quality of the surface of the material. Mosaic technique allows the creation of work where the texture takes on importance, and becomes a value in itself. However, this component is always associated with the tile in that it is concerned with its material and chromatic characteristics, both of which are inseparable. The textures become a tool for emphasizing the idea you wish to communicate, through creating contrasts, separating areas, or relating parts of the work. The textural effects are achieved by using different materials or manipulating one material by cutting, snipping, or other interventions to create similar pieces with diverse textures.

The combination of volumetric pieces contrasted with flat ceramic, textured ceramic, and glass are some of the possibilities for using textures when making mosaics. Detail of the deck in Can Roca, in Esparraguerra, Barcelona. Lívia Garreta, 1989. Photograph by Toni Coll.

Reflection

Reflections can be specular or diffuse. A specular reflection is produced when light hits a polished surface such as a mirror. Mirrors and other materials allow this aspect to be introduced into the work. A mirror, as a component of mosaics, is used to create interesting contrasts, although its use in a work next to other materials can cause problems, therefore, it can become a very useful recourse, and it will work perfectly well if it is used alone, but it can create problems in reading the design if it is not correctly combined with the other materials. The mirror catches the attention of the viewer, creating a bright reflective surface that strongly attracts attention; it also reflects the surroundings, introducing images of the outside world into the work, which can enrich the mosaic, but also generate conflicting forms.

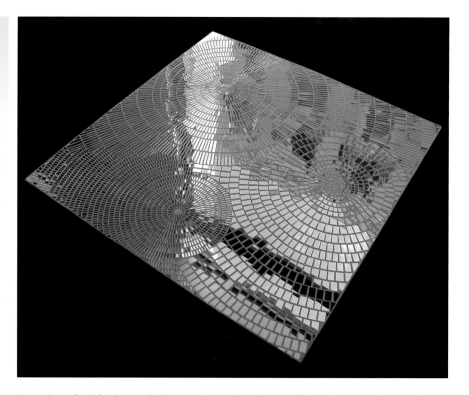

A mosaic made with mirrors, which create interesting reflecting effects. The general pattern for placing the pieces is circular, combining three circular elements that contrast because of the sizes of the pieces. *Table,* Damien Morrison, 2002.

Sheen, Shade, and Transparency

Sheen is the specular reflection of light, although in this case it is covered separately from mirrors, because as a material it has some specific characteristics that make it different from the others. Sheen, a counterpoint to shade, is defined by the qualities of the material that is used. Glass, glass tiles, and glazed ceramics have smooth, vitrified surfaces where light, when it reflects, makes the work shine. Enamel tiles also have a vitreous surface, although it is irregular, not continuous, and textured, where light hits to create interesting reflections that add to the texture and other components of this material. Unpolished marble and stone, and unglazed ceramic have matte surfaces that contrast with the reflective ones.

Glass and some plastics allow us to introduce transparency into the work, creating contrasts against opaque areas or pieces and adding depth to the surface of the mosaic.

The top of this chimney is covered with green glass mosaic work, adding sheen. The color and qualities of the glass contrast with the mosaic below, at the same time highlighting the architectural element that evokes the plant world. View of one of the chimneys of the Palacio Güell in Barcelona, work of Antoni Gaudí, 1886–1891.

Reflections and transparencies are combined in this mosaic. The pieces of transparent glass (located in the central motif) add depth and contrast with the surface reflection of the vitreous ceramic around the outside. Philippa Beveridge, 2004.

Volume

Today, mosaic is seen as a very versatile medium of expression in which it is possible to integrate attributes that historically did not form part of its traditional language. The enormous interest awakened by this art has carried with it a search for new approaches and the inclusion of attributes typical of other disciplines, such as volume. Its resurgent popularity, like that experienced by other artistic media since the 1980s, has turned into a search for new creative approaches and into research in formal and technical innovations. Volume in mosaics is defined by two elements: the support and the pieces. Today, it is possible to use supports of any desired form; their limitations are based on the ability to correctly attach the pieces and on the stability of the work. However, the most interesting effects are those made strictly in the creation of the mosaic, that is, based on the pieces. The use of pieces with form or ones cut from them offer a limitless number of approaches with which it is possible to create any form in three dimensions or integrate volumes into the mosaic. The inclusion of three-dimensional attributes in the work gives it qualities similar to those of sculpture, specifically those of relief work and creating chiaroscuro effects. The play of shadows and illuminated areas forms part of the work and enriches it. Mosaic also holds important possibilities for the field of freestanding sculpture, being an ideal medium for covering sculptural surfaces.

Outdoor planter. An example of mosaics applied to a volume. Work by Lívia Garreta, 1994. Photograph by Balta Quesada.

In this example we can see the architect's intention of emphasizing the curved forms of the wall with mosaics. The curves, or rounded surfaces, have been covered with white mosaic. This color is visually expansive and highlights the volume. The flat areas are covered with dark-colored mosaics to emphasize the play of volumes and chiaroscuro. Parque Güell in Barcelona, work of Antoni Gaudí, 1900–1914.

Movement

Movement in mosaics can be indicated by using different techniques that are used alone or in combination to make this aspect stand out. It can be suggested by the placement pattern of the pieces, creating wavy, fanned, or circular arrangements. These patterns in the composition can be juxtaposed against areas with structured arrangements to create contrasts between an area that suggests movement and one that transmits a static feeling to emphasize the desired value. The directionality of the placement, or better said, the combinations and changes in direction, also suggest a sense of movement. Tonal color transitions and the possibilities offered by the placement and form of color pieces are techniques that create effects of movement. Finally, it is worth pointing out the possibilities offered by the shape and sizes of the color pieces. The ones with irregular forms, with circular or wavy shapes, communicate dynamic attributes that can be used to suggest movement.

The movement of the fish in the central motif, achieved by juxtaposing two facing sinuous shapes, is complemented by the background effect. The placement of the dark pieces, which establishes a gradation from above, where there are few, to the bottom, placed with an equal number of white pieces, results in a chromatic rhythm that creates movement. Philippa Beveridge, 1992–1993.

Gaudí's interest in reinforcing the sense of movement in his architecture with mosaic can be appreciated in this detail. Casa Milá, also known as La Pedrera, in Barcelona, work of Antoni Gaudí, 1906–1910.

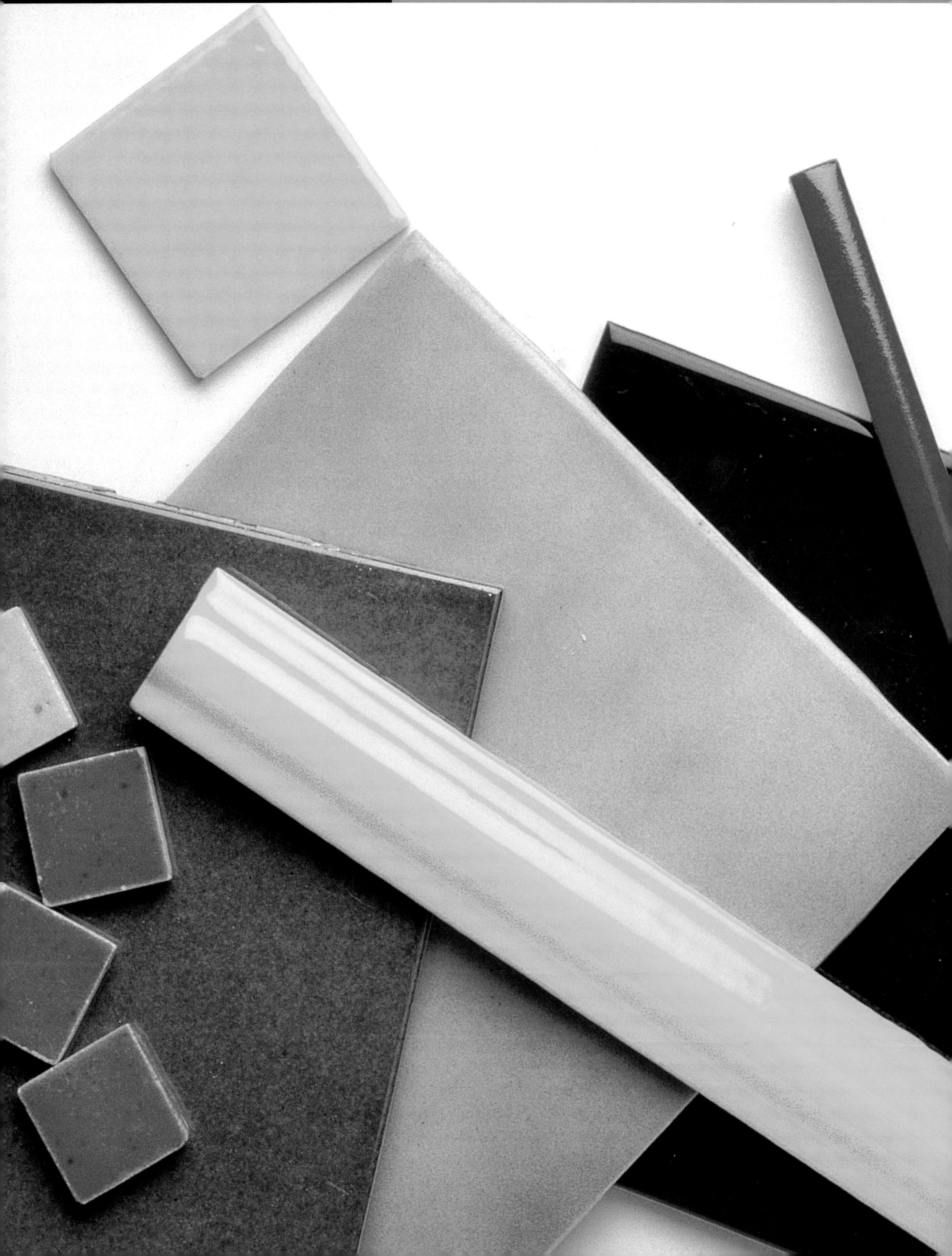

Materials and Tools

Artistic disciplines always require the application of different technical and creative processes. Implicit in any art is the use of diverse techniques, some of which are very different from each other. The art of mosaic is no exception. The creative process and the making of a mosaic require the use of techniques typical of other art forms such as drawing or painting, and from trades such as masonry, among others. There is a wide range of such elements that make up the list of different materials and tools that can possibly be used.

Materials

Mosaic work requires very specific materials, some of which are traditional, used for creating mosaics throughout the history of the art. When used in new ways and combined with new materials, these allow us to create works that reinterpret this art.

In this chapter we explain the characteristics and the uses of these materials, the traditional and the new, to create pieces and tiles and the support, as well as the entire process, from the design to the finish.

Basic Materials

The basic materials are those used to acquire or make the pieces that create the mosaic and those used for the support. The materials for making tiles or pieces can be of natural origin, such as stones and seashells, or artificial, such as glass, ceramic, and plastic. When it comes to supports, it should be pointed out that mosaics can be created on a wide range of different surfaces, including new materials, for example, certain plastics and gypsum wall panels.

Different marbles (A), granite (B), and slate (C).

Pieces

• Stones

Stones and stone materials were the elements used to create the first mosaics. The diversity of these materials offers a wide spectrum of colors, textures, and qualities to choose from, the most common being marble, granite, and slate. They are enormously resistant and can be used to create very durable and beautiful mosaics. Pebbles or river stones, for example, are very durable, and are available in different sizes, forms, and colors, making them ideal for this use.

River stones and pebbles.

• Glass

Glass is also a commonly used material for creating mosaics. Its unique characteristics and properties influence the way it should be cut. Any glass can be used for making mosaics, and it can even be used as the raw material for making pieces (tiles) in the workshop.

Glass and mirrored glass.

Glass tiles with laminated gold and silver.

In addition to glass and mirrored glass, we must include enamel (*smalti*) and glass tiles. Enamel tiles are small opaque pieces of glass paste of different colors. Their particular characteristics and the large range of available colors make them a very attractive material for creating mosaics; the major drawback is their high cost. Glass tiles are industrial pieces of glass. They are sold attached to heavy paper with a water-soluble adhesive, forming panels or pieces in squares. They require some previous preparation, consisting of soaking the panel in hot water until the paper comes off and the adhesive is softened.

Commercial pieces of glass (A), and plastic (B).

A

B

Enamel tiles (*smalti*).

Glass tiles.

Glazed ceramics: borders (A), wall tiles (B), floor tiles (C), and small tiles (D).

• Ceramic

Ceramic is a versatile material, very durable, easy to cut and work; it comes in a wide range of forms and finishes, and it is less expensive than some stones and glass tile. This makes it one of the most widely used materials for making mosaics. It is possible to make tiles or pieces from floor tile, wall tile, or shaped ceramic, whether fragmented or whole. Borders, frames, and other flat pieces can also be used.

Glazed ceramic, also known as varnished or enameled ceramic, are pieces that have been covered with a layer of glaze to protect it, creating a smooth and vitreous surface that waterproofs it. It is appropriate for outdoor mosaics and those that will be in constant use.

Unglazed ceramic has no protective layer. It can be colored or have natural color (terra-cotta, for example). It is porous, which limits its use to certain kinds of mosaics.

Stoneware ceramic tiles are made from this resistant and impermeable material, which is opaque, heavy, and dense. The tiles are very thin, very durable, and hard, in shades of opaque color.

Pieces and fragments of ceramic objects.

Unglazed ceramic floor tiles (A), and stoneware ceramic tiles (B).

• Other Materials

In addition to the materials we have covered up to now are other, less traditional ones. There are limits because of the technical characteristics of each one, their potential for working, and their durability. Materials that can be used include natural materials such as seashells, and man-made ones such as plastic and certain metal alloys.

Seashells.

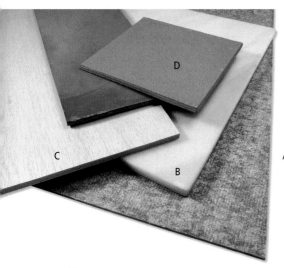

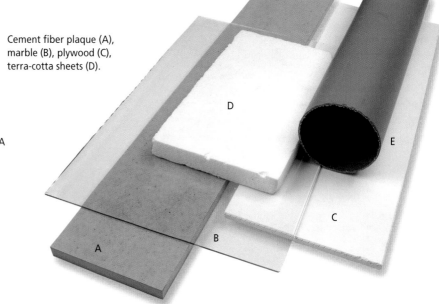

Cement fiber plaque (A), marble (B), plywood (C), terra-cotta sheets (D).

Medium density plank (A), glass (B), laminated gypsum board (C), expanded polystyrene (D), polyvinyl chloride, PVC, tube (E).

Supports

A mosaic can be created on any support, as long as it has a solid and reliable surface and the appropriate adhesive and mortar are used (see "Placement"). Therefore it is possible to place them on walls, whether covered with tile, brick, cement, or gypsum panels, and on cement and tiled floors. They can also be used on wood panels (solid, plywood, and MDF), furniture, structural elements (beams, for example), and elements such as doors. Add to this glass (windows and objects), marble, terra-cotta (planters, urns), and objects made of polyvinyl chloride (PVC).

Commonly Used Materials

Commonly used materials are those that are employed during the process of creating the mosaic. They are used for making the design, creating the pieces, constructing the mosaic, grouting, and later, cleaning and applying the finish, if there is one. These materials become indispensable in creating the work, and complement the basic materials during the entire creative process. Now we will explain their main characteristics, grouping them according to their use.

Materials for Designing and Provisional Supports

• Design
The design is generally made with pencil or charcoal on paper. Once the motif is selected, a sketch is made on paper or cardboard, coloring it with any number of techniques: pencil, pastel, watercolor, etc. Once the design is finished it may

be necessary to reduce the form to lines to transfer the motif to the support; sketchbook paper is used as a sort of carbon paper. Carbon or graphite paper is used to directly transfer motifs of medium size or simple forms.

• Provisional Supports
Provisional supports are used during the process of creating certain mosaics, attaching the pieces to them to act as a temporary surface on which the work is assembled. Once the mosaic is attached to the final support, the provisional one is removed. Wrapping paper and acetate are the most popular provisional supports.

Strong and heavy wrapping paper commonly used for shipping things is used for direct and indirect placement techniques for floor mosaics. The acetate sheet is transparent and is used for the double indirect placement technique, by placing it over the original design to attach the pieces and tiles according to the final placement.

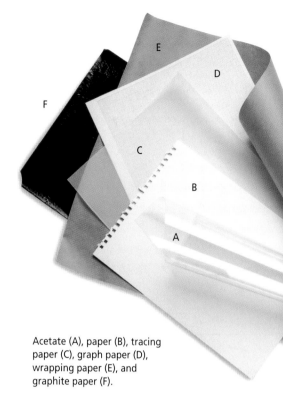

Acetate (A), paper (B), tracing paper (C), graph paper (D), wrapping paper (E), and graphite paper (F).

Materials for sketching and design: pencils, markers, wax crayons, and watercolors.

Materials for Making Pieces

• For Polishing Cut Pieces

A dressing stone is used for the final polishing of cut pieces of glass and ceramic. It is very useful for eliminating jagged edges and excess material on pieces that have been cut. It can also be used to sharpen tools.

• For Pieces of Glass

Many different materials can be used to make pieces of laminated glass, adding color to adhesives, and making inclusions. The two-part adhesives that are used to join the glass pieces can be colored by adding pigments and paints, for example, powdered pigments or oil paint. Inclusions are made by placing the selected material on a layer of adhesive after it is applied to one of the glass pieces. You can use metallic laminations (gold, silver, or copper, or alloys that look like them), or paper that can be printed or drawn on, and even photocopies. Other pieces can be made by painting them with special paint for glass.

Dressing stone.

Glass paint (A), oil paint (B), acrylic paint (C), Metalic lamination (D), photocopy (E).

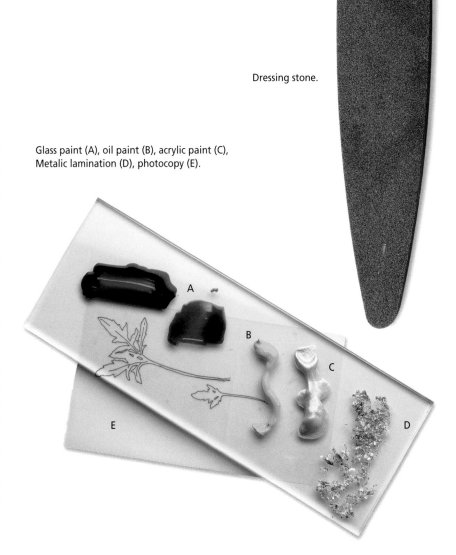

• Acid-Etched Glass

Making pieces of acid-etched glass requires acid cream and a material for making reserves, such as a sheet of adhesive plastic. The acid cream is a chemical preparation (based on sulfuric acid, sodium bifluoride, hydrofluoric acid, ammonia, and other components) with the consistency of a liquid cream that is used to shade the glass; it makes a finish similar to that of industrial etched work. The shading is produced by the chemical action of the acids in the cream on the surface of the glass, which results in a surface layer that is translucent and of a whitish color. It is very important to follow the manufacturer's instructions referring to its use and protection.

The sheet of adhesive plastic (generally transparent, although it is available in different colors) has a strong adhesive on one of its sides protected by a sheet of paper. After removing it, the plastic is permanently attached to any surface. It is often used for covering books.

Adhesive plastic sheet and acid cream.

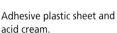

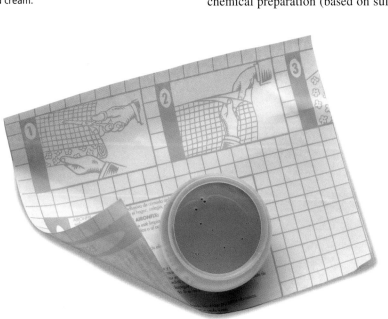

• Clays

The use of new materials allows us make special pieces in the workshop based on the particular needs of each mosaic. Modeling clay is a material with characteristics similar to those of natural clay (in color, texture, and look) that does not require firing. For school and hobby use, it is used in the same way as natural clay and when it is dry it can be sanded with sandpaper, drilled, painted, and varnished.

Polymer clay is worked just like modeling clay and is baked in a domestic oven at 250°F (130°C) for 15 minutes (the time may vary according to manufacturer), with the pieces set on a nonporous surface. It is available in a large variety of colors and finishes. After it has been baked and cooled, it can be polished, sanded, drilled, ground, cut, and even painted with water-based acrylic paint.

Sandpaper and wire.

Polymer clay.

In certain cases, different materials, among them wire, can be added to the pieces of shaped clay.

Materials for Construction

• Adhesives

Adhesives are used to attach the pieces to the final support or for attaching them to the provisional support, as well as for making pieces in the workshop. In each case the appropriate adhesive must be chosen according to the mosaic, the support, and where it will be placed. Generally, white glue, silicone, the adhesive for expanded polystyrene, or cyanoacrilate are used to attach the pieces to the final support; methylcellulose glue is used for temporary supports, and two-part adhesives are reserved for making pieces in the workshop.

White glue, or carpenter's glue, is a polyvinyl acetate adhesive (PVA), appropriate for attaching mosaics to wood surfaces and plastic screen. Somewhat slow drying, it allows small adjustments; it is white but becomes transparent when it dries. Silicone (semisynthetic polymer) will hold pieces to any surface, and is mainly used for mosaics on glass (transparent silicone) and on polyvinyl chlorate (PVC). It is

necessary to use a special adhesive to attach pieces and tiles to an expanded polystyrene panel, since some products can degrade it and cause damage and/or the emission of noxious fumes. Cyanoacrilate adhesive is liquid and not very viscous; it adheres instantly and makes a very strong bond, although it dries completely in 24 hours. It is used for small area touchups.

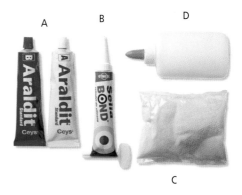

Two-part resin adhesive (A), silicone (B), unmixed methylcellulose (C), white PVA glue (D).

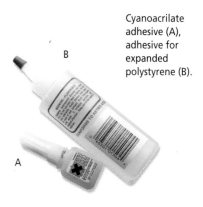

Cyanoacrilate adhesive (A), adhesive for expanded polystyrene (B).

• Mortars

Mortars are compounds composed of cement and other materials with water that are used to attach the pieces to the support or make a support on which the mosaic will be placed. Mortar can be made in the workshop (see "Preparations") or purchased ready for use. Two types are used in mosaic work: bricklayer's mortar and cement adhesive. The latter is used for attaching pieces to ceramic supports, gypsum wall panels, and fiber cement walls, floors, and surfaces. Adhesive cement is available in different varieties for the wall or floor, in black or white.

Mortar with latex is used for attaching mosaics to wood surfaces. This is a milky, water-based mixture of synthetic resins that improves the adhesion of the mortar to the wood and imparts plasticity to the mixture. It is possible to purchase mortars with latex, but preparing them in the studio reduces the expense.

• Auxiliary Materials

Auxiliary construction materials are those used for making molds and reinforcing the supports. Different materials are used for making molds, which are the frames where the mortar is deposited, for example, wood slats (connected with nails or screws) or metal pieces (such as a table frame). In every case it is very important to apply a release agent to keep the mortar from sticking to the frame. Common release agents are petroleum jelly and soap (natural soap dissolved in water). To support the mold a resistant metal screen is used to reinforce the mosaic, then it is covered with mortar. A plastic or fiberglass screen is used for mosaics made with the direct technique that are inset in a wall.

The mortar is covered with a plastic sheet for at least 72 hours so that it will cure correctly.

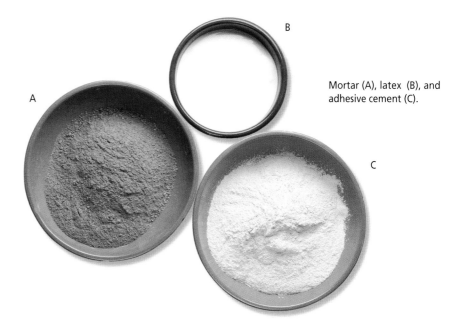

Mortar (A), latex (B), and adhesive cement (C).

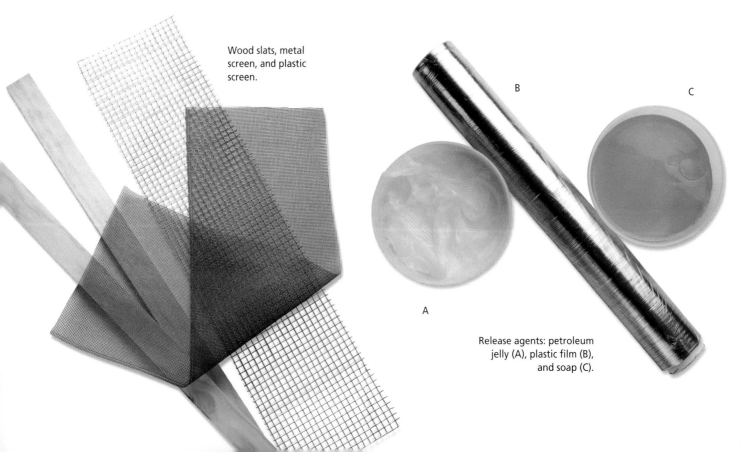

Wood slats, metal screen, and plastic screen.

Release agents: petroleum jelly (A), plastic film (B), and soap (C).

Material for Grouting

Grout is used for rejoining the mosaic pieces. It is mixed with water and used to fill the joints between the pieces and tiles. Different kinds are sold, normal and with an antifungal additive to prevent mold. It can be colored by adding powdered pigments (when it is dry) or with dyes (after it is mixed with water).

Water-based paint can be used to change the color of the joints after the mosaic is finished. Using a brush, the grout is painted with watercolor, acrylic, or tempera.

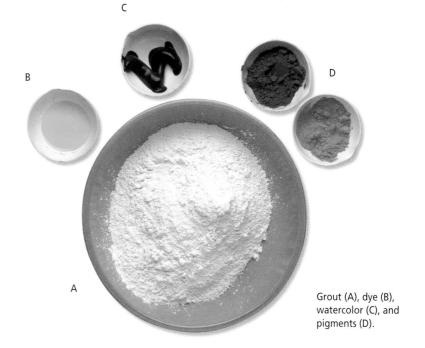

Grout (A), dye (B), watercolor (C), and pigments (D).

Materials for Cleaning

Different commonly used materials such as paper towels, rags, cotton, and scouring pads, are used for removing traces of mortar during the creation of the mosaic and for the final cleanup of the grout and paint.

Paper towels, sponge, scouring pad, toothpicks, and cotton.

Materials for Finishing

Wax or varnish is applied to cover the mosaic in cases when it is necessary to give it a layer of protection.

The wax is applied to the surface and buffed, when it has dried, with a cotton rag. Waxing imparts a deep, satiny sheen; however, it is somewhat fragile, tending to accumulate dust, and it turns white when it comes in contact with water or excess humidity. Varnish, usually with an acrylic base, leaves a fine, even layer, and is a very durable finish. You can choose varnishes that are satin or gloss, with color, and resistant to damaging atmospheric agents.

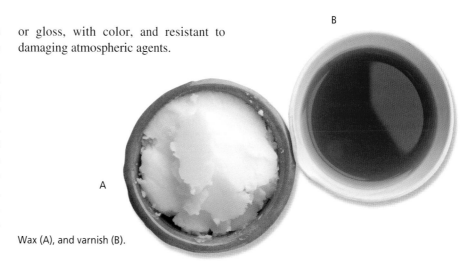

Wax (A), and varnish (B).

Tools

The tools that are used in making mosaics are as varied as the different processes that are applied. Most of them are used for other artistic techniques, such as working in stained glass or masonry. Some, however, are specific to mosaics. Following are shown the basic tools for carrying out the mosaic projects in this book, grouped according to their primary use.

Basic Tools

The basic tools are considered to be the ones that are used directly in the creation of mosaics. They cut, score, and polish the pieces and tiles, as well as cutting and preparing the supports. Also, those that are used for mixing and applying the adhesives, mortars, and grout, and those used for assembling the pieces and the mosaic.

For Cutting, Scoring, and Polishing

• Cold Chisel
This is a useful tool, with a triangular section, a sharp edge at the top and a cylindrical shape at the bottom. The latter is inserted in a support, a tree trunk with a box or wood receptacle that serves as a sort of a stand. The wooden box catches the fragments of the pieces that are cut.

• Tile Cutter
This is used for cutting tile, and sometimes for cutting and breaking up very thick pieces of glass. The cut is made with a small disk of hardened metal that is attached to a handle that slides between two fixed guides.

Cold chisel.

Cold chisel mounted on a tree trunk as a base with a box for catching the fragments of cut stone. The cut is made with a hammer with a sharp head.

Tile cutter.

Pliers.

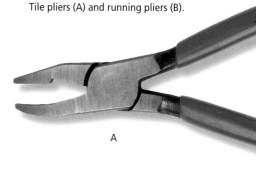

Tile pliers (A) and running pliers (B).

A

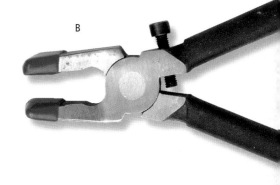

B

• Tile Cutter

This hardened steel tool has two points attached by a bolt so they will close with a biting action. Some have small cutting wheels attached at the cutting points. As the cutting edge of the wheels wears down, they are given a slight turn, so the tool will continue cutting accurately. They are used for cutting stone, ceramic, and tile.

• Glass Cutters and Tile Scoring Stylus

Cutters, or roulettes, are tools that consist of a handle, usually wood, with a cutter at one end. This is a metal piece with a small wheel inside that cuts as it rotates. They are used to mark a line that weakens the glass.

The scoring stylus is used to mark a scored line on the surface of glazed tile, which makes it easier to cut. It is a metal instrument similar to a pencil that has a metal point for scoring.

• Running Pliers and Tile Pliers

Running pliers have jaws that are covered with pieces of plastic that are used to help separate scored glass. Once the glass has been marked, the pliers are placed on the scored line and pressure is applied to them until the pieces separate.

Tile pliers are used as an auxiliary tool for separating cut pieces and cutting very small pieces.

• Expanded Polystyrene Cutter

A special tool is used for cutting expanded polystyrene (EPS) or Styrofoam. The cutter consists of a handle, which holds the batteries and a switch, and a frame that holds a thin wire. When the cutter is switched on the wire becomes hot, enabling it to cut the expanded polystyrene quickly and cleanly. A more basic method of cutting this material consists of using a cutting blade that has been heated.

Expanded polystyrene cutter.

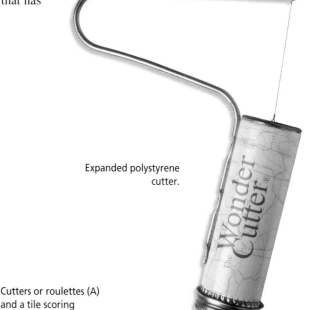

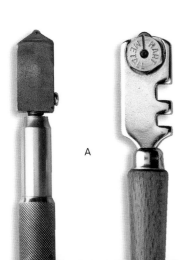

A

B

Cutters or roulettes (A) and a tile scoring stylus (B).

• Other Tools

A chisel can be used for splitting layers of slate after they are separated from larger pieces. A saw is very useful for cutting gypsum panels, and if you have a sheet of wood, for making supports from it. Wire cutters can be used for cutting and shaping parts of some mosaic elements, Christmas ornaments, for example.

A knife is useful as a spatula for separating the finished mosaic from its provisional support, and scissors and a craft knife with replaceable blades for cutting forms and patterns to serve as guides in making mosaics.

For Mixing and Applying

• Scrapers

Scrapers are used for mixing, dispensing, applying, and leveling mortar. Metal scrapers and particularly those used by painters can be used for mixing and applying small quantities as well as for leveling large surfaces. A plasterer's trowel can be useful for some applications, but the plastic ones are most practical. A notched trowel is best for preparing the bed of mortar for both the direct and indirect techniques for floor mosaics. The surface relief of the mortar enhances the union of the pieces.

• Spatulas

Metal spatulas are used for handling and applying mortar and for cleaning and removing traces of it or of grout. To remove grout deposited on the pieces after the joints have been filled, you can use wooden spatulas that will not mar the surfaces. In certain cases it is necessary to use special metal spatulas to remove more resistant bits.

Wire cutters (A), knife (B), chisel (C), and a saw for gypsum panels (D).

Scissors and craft knife with disposable blades.

Brush (A), wooden spatula (B), plastic scrapers (C), notched trowel (D), painter's scraper (E), metal scrapers (F), metal spatula (G).

• Brushes

These are used for both mixing and applying grout and for applying paint to color the joints of a finished mosaic.

• Containers

Mosaic work requires the use of different containers for mixing and making preparations. A mason's bucket is very useful for mixing mortar.

Bucket and containers.

Brushes.

For Handling and Placing

Tweezers and an awl are very useful for handling and placing small pieces. Tweezers also allow you to place pieces very precisely into small spaces. The awl is used for making small adjustments and fixing imperfections after the

Tweezers.

Awl.

mosaic is removed from the provisional support, as well as for cleaning bits of mortar out of very narrow joints or mortar from corners.

Auxiliary Tools

These are items that are used for secondary processes and for safety. This becomes a most important aspect of the work, and it is essential to use the correct safety equipment when required. The rest of the tools are used in the preparation and elaboration of the mosaic.

Safety

All of these products and materials must be used according to the manufacturer's instructions and following correct protective guidelines. Leather gloves are used to protect your hands when manipulating and cutting large stones. Eye protection must always be used when making cuts. When cutting or sawing certain materials a dust mask should also be used. Latex gloves are useful for protecting your skin from chemical irritants.

Other Tools

• Instruments for Measuring and Leveling
These are used for taking measurements and as guides for marking the design and support when transferring the drawing with a grid. Levels are used for checking that the mosaic and its support have level surfaces.

• For Striking
Mallets and hammers are used for striking the framed support holding the mortar to cause bubbles to come to the surface. They are also used for leveling pieces and tiles with the help of a piece of wood or a slat. Hammers also are used to break tiles to create the characteristic look of the pieces.

• For Cleaning
In addition to the items already mentioned can be added synthetic brushes for personal use (toothbrushes) for removing traces of mortar and grout from the surface of the mosaic.

Leather gloves, dust mask, latex glove, and safety glasses.

Mallet and hammers.

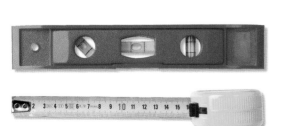

Levels and
tape measure.

3 Techniques

Mosaic, like any other artistic discipline, requires a creative process. This is explicit in the different stages of the work: design, preparation, cutting and creation of the pieces, and the techniques for assembling and finishing. Creating mosaics does not entail great technical difficulties, although it is a bit arduous, which means it is essential to reflect and study before beginning to work. At the same time, this art has much to offer in the way of forms and techniques that can be used for decorating and covering any material. The use of innovative materials and the creation of pieces in the workshop further enhance the wide range of creative possibilities.

In this chapter we explain the basic fundamentals of every stage of the process, paying special attention to the aspects that allow the most creative freedom.

The Project

Like all artistic disciplines, the creation of mosaic works requires a preliminary design. Its function is to organize the necessary previous thinking required of all creating and to act as a guide during the different phases of the work.

Once the main techniques and approaches are learned, the art of mosaics does not present any particular difficulties, although it is a laborious process requiring a lot of work. For this reason a preliminary design becomes indispensable.

Designing

The first step in the project consists of making pencil sketches of the idea. The selected motif could be created based on numerous approaches that are suggested by different sources of information (see the section "Sources of Inspiration") or by using the materials as a point of departure, since in this there are no limitations. The only possible advice for those who wish to learn this art form is to choose simple motifs for the first projects. Later, as progress is made through practice, and with a little experience, you can attempt more complicated projects.

The different components that play a part in the creation of a motif or design must be studied before beginning the work. These are the outline, or silhouette of the motif, the line, form (which in objects is three-dimensional, but after being applied in the design and the mosaic ends up being two-dimensional), and the color or the tone, and the quality of the surface. The way the motif is applied in the design depends on the component that you wish to emphasize. A motif dominated by form will not be designed the same way as one in which the colors are emphasized.

The design is not just limited to a sketch, although some artists create very elaborate mosaics based on superficial color sketches. However, a detailed drawing minimizes errors and guarantees that the mosaic, once finished, will not present any problems.

The first step in creating a design is to choose the subject of the mosaic. In this case, a charcoal drawing was made of some flowers (lilies) from life. *Lily*, by Philippa Beveridge, 1995.

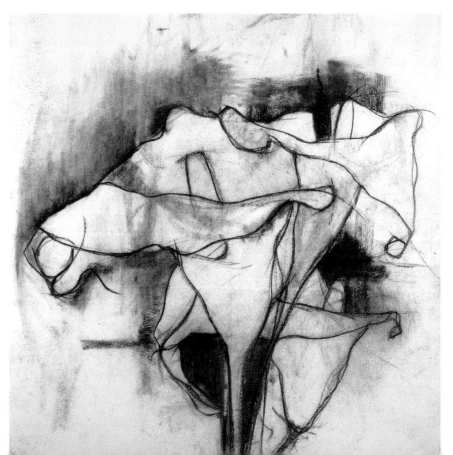

The Sketch

The sketch will be the design in color including more or less detailed elements of the project. It is made smaller than the final mosaic, usually in pencil or charcoal, although it could also be a photograph, a tracing, or even a photocopy, from which a full-sized version of the motif can be made.

After the original sketch is made, it may be necessary to reduce it to lines that indicate and define the parts of the subject. This can be done by making a tracing using graphite paper, with a graphic approach such as a photocopy, or by transferring the drawing by making a grid on the sketch and on the original surface. Some of these approaches will be seen in detail in various projects in the following chapters. An example of the use of line sketches taken from color designs is mosaics that are made using the indirect placement technique. With this system the mosaic is created opposite from the way it will look once it is finished and mounted, so the provisional support (see "Indirect Placement") should present the mirror image of the design motif.

The designs are created according to the particular requirements of each project, which are different for each mosaic. When creating the design, you must take into account the parameters of the project, for example, the materials that will be available, their characteristics, colors, possible pieces, and limitations, as well as the possible methods of assembly. When the mosaic is finished, it will differ from the sketch in color, since the colors can vary according to the selected materials, but not when it comes to the basic formal attributes. Of course, it is possible to make variations during the process of actually assembling the mosaic, but they should never completely alter the original design.

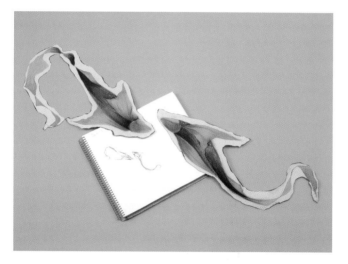

Sketch and design of two elements that form part of a larger work; in this case a wall completely decorated with mosaics. Work by Philippa Beveridge, 1993.

Design for a decorative panel, watercolor on paper. Work by Philippa Beveridge, 1993.

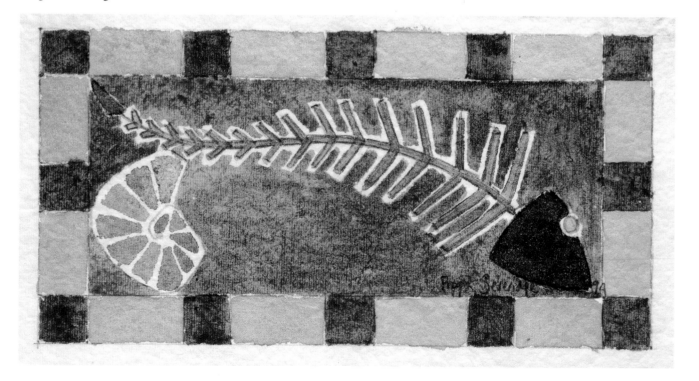

Preliminary and final sketches for *Earth*, a mosaic in the series "The Four Elements," by Philippa Beveridge, 1996. Notice that, in this case, the preliminary sketch was made using images taken from an image file and attached to the paper.

The finished mosaic. The forms and dimensions of the final work match those of the original design.

A view of the stairway where the mosaic is located.

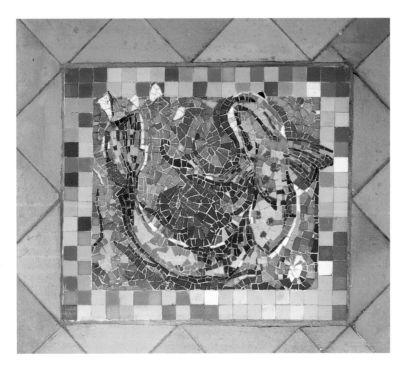

Preliminary and final sketches for *Water*, a mosaic in the series "The Four Elements," by Philippa Beveridge, 1996.

In this case, the mosaic was finally located in a place that was somewhat smaller than originally planned, making it necessary to vary the proportions of the frame and the background of the composition.

Preliminary sketch for *Air* and final sketch for *Fire*, both mosaics from the series "The Four Elements," by Philippa Beveridge, 1996.

Angled step decorated with the mosaic *Fire*.

Landing decorated with the mosaic *Air*.

Cutting and Preparing the Pieces

Mosaics can be created using commercial pieces or tiles, although in most cases special pieces are required, cut according to the particular requirements of the project. Creativity extends to the possibilities presented in cutting the many materials that can be used; therefore, it is essential to know the different cutting and preparation techniques, which vary according to the materials.

Cutting Stone

Stone materials, because of their characteristics, require certain cutting techniques. Although they are somewhat laborious, they are not complicated, since they consist of simply striking with a hammer on the cold chisel to make the desired cuts. It is also possible to make cuts using pliers, although this method works only with pebbles or very thin slabs.

Cutting with the Cold Chisel

A cold chisel must be used for cutting hard materials. It can be used to make medium to small pieces by just cutting or breaking the stone at the desired place.

The stone is held so that the place where you wish to make the cut rests on the edge of the chisel while it is held with one hand. The other hand strikes it with a hammer so that its edge or point lands on the same vertical plane as the edge of the cold chisel. The blow should be hard and clean to break the stone in two.

The cold chisel may be used to cut thin pieces of marble. Notice that the edges of the hammer and chisel are on the same plane.

Pebbles and river stones are easily cut into smaller pieces.

It is also useful for cutting tesserae.

Cutting with Pliers

In some cases it is also possible to cut some stones using tile pliers. Their use, however, is restricted to cutting thin stone material and pebbles. Strips of stone slabs that have been machine cut in a specialized shop can be easily cut with such nippers.

Flat pebbles and river stones can be fragmented to make very specific shapes. They are cut by placing the jaws of the pliers at the edge of the stone and applying pressure. The pliers should never be placed at the center of the stone, since it would be impossible to apply enough force to make the cut.

Pebbles can also be cut with the pliers. Notice how the jaws of the tool are placed at the edge of the stone.

Cutting Glass

With glass, the cut is made by fracturing, or by traction when it has reached the limit of its resistance. To cut it a mark is made on it with a glass cutter or roulette to create a line of weakness; this will fracture when pressure is applied (mechanically).

Cutting glass, although not difficult at all, requires skill, which can be acquired with a little practice.

Glass Tiles

Making tiles from glass is a very easy process. The cuts, which are always straight, are scored with the glass cutter and a straight edge, and the fracturing is carried out using pliers or running pliers.

1. The line is marked for scoring. One hand firmly holds the straight edge on the glass, while the cutter is manipulated with the other. It is moved without applying too much pressure, perpendicular to the surface of the glass, using the straight edge as a guide. The scored line should always be made by moving the cutter toward you.

2. The running pliers are aligned with the scored line as seen in the photograph. The glass can easily be cut cleanly by applying pressure with them.

3. Equally spaced scored lines are marked on the strip to create similarly sized tiles.

4. Then the glass pieces are separated with the pliers. The strip is held with one hand, with the fingers on the scored line of the next tile to be cut. The other hand holds the pliers, their ends located near the scored line, and the tile is then easily snapped off.

Shapes

Cutting pieces with compound shapes and curvilinear sides does not differ substantially from cutting straight lines, although the process does involve a greater number of steps.

Creating pieces with irregular shapes requires a pattern to serve as a guide for marking the glass. The cuts must be made in several stages until the desired shape is achieved, as we explain below.

1. The pattern is placed in the desired position on the glass, and held firmly with one hand. The other hand, holding a glass cutter perpendicular to the glass surface, scores the shape on the glass leaving 3/16 to 1/4 inch (1–1 1/2 cm) between the scored line and the cardboard, as seen in the photograph.

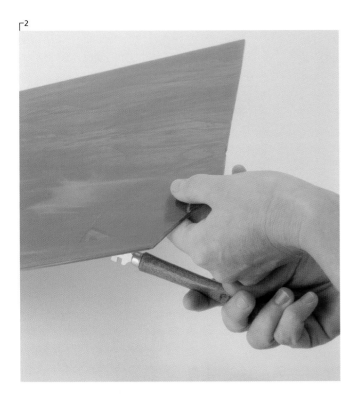

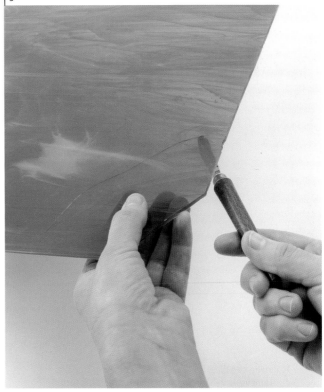

2. Since we are working with a large piece of glass with some wavy forms, the cut is made with the utmost care to avoid unwanted breaks. To do this, the outside part of the shape is broken off where it meets the glass sheet. The center of the piece is held with one hand while the other very lightly taps the underside of the scored line with the end of the glass cutter.

3. Continue tapping lightly under the scored line following the shape of the piece. The sheet of glass will separate from the cut-out piece.

4. The inside convex part of the glass is snapped off with pliers. Notice that the cut glass is somewhat larger than the pattern, which makes it necessary to cut it a second time

5. To do this, a new line is scored, closely following the edge of the pattern.

6. The scored lines are broken with pliers. The result is a piece of glass shaped like the pattern.

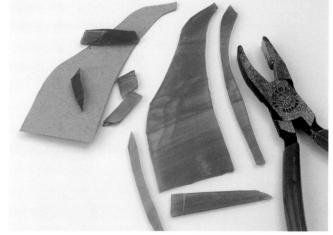

7. Finally, the glass is polished with a dressing stone to remove any sharp edges and give it the final form.

Pieces of Laminated Glass

Pieces of laminated glass created in the studio (see "Making Pieces in the Studio") have certain characteristics that determine how they are cut. These pieces are made with two layers of glass glued together with a film of resin, so cutting will be done in two stages.

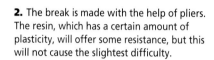

1. The cutting line is scored on one side of the piece, as seen in the photograph. The scored lines on both sides must line up to ensure a perfect break. It is very useful to mark both ends of the cut with a permanent marker by holding the piece up against the light, since the lines will be references for making the scored line on the other side of the piece.

2. The break is made with the help of pliers. The resin, which has a certain amount of plasticity, will offer some resistance, but this will not cause the slightest difficulty.

Cutting Commercial Tile

Manufactured tile is available in a large number of materials, qualities, and formats. However, on many occasions it will have to be cut to create pieces whose shapes and sizes will correctly fill the requirements of each project.

1. In this case we will use an enamel tile (*smalti*) as an example. The cut is made by holding the cutting heads perpendicular to the tile and forcefully squeezing the pliers.

2. When cutting glass tiles they and the pliers' cutting wheels are placed on the slightly closed palm of the other hand to keep from losing any pieces that might fly into the air.

Cutting pliers let you create pieces of the shape and size required by your mosaics.

Cutting Tiles and Ceramic Pieces

Ceramic materials open up a wide range of possibilities for creating mosaics. Wall tiles, and by extension, all ceramic tiles, offer a limitless repertory of colors, textures, and quality, besides being materials that are easy to cut and very reasonably priced.

Straight-Sided Pieces

A tile cutter is used for making straight cuts on tiles and flat ceramic pieces. The cutting wheel scores the cutting line on the surface of the ceramic, which breaks apart when pressure is applied to it with the lever. The scored line is made by moving the cutting wheel from outside to inside, pushing the handle away from you while applying light pressure.

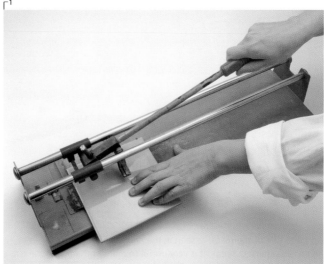

1. The ceramic piece is placed in the cutter so that one of its sides is braced against the stopper. It is held firmly with one hand while the other grasps the handle of the lever that controls the cutting wheel.

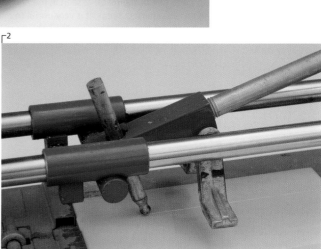

2. The cutting wheel is placed on the bottom edge of the ceramic. Then the line is scored by applying pressure to the handle while it is moved forward, pushing the cutting wheel against the ceramic until arriving at the other side.

3. The tile is snapped along the line by applying light pressure with the lever. This results in a straight and clean break.

4. Small tiles are made by cutting up strips.

Fragmenting

The fragmenting technique, sometimes called *pique assiette*, consists of breaking the ceramic to create irregular pieces of varying sizes that will fit back together. Fragmenting was a technique employed by the Catalan architect Antonio Gaudí and his collaborators (who called it *trencadis*) to cover curved and wavy façades, roofs, and exterior elements. Its use allows any surface, no matter how complicated, to be covered with ceramic.

The ceramic is broken by striking the back with a hammer. The side with the color or glaze should never be struck, since this can cause spalling, chipping, and even cracking over the entire surface.

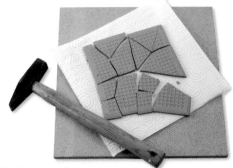

A hammer is used to fragment the ceramic piece (in this case, a floor tile). The ceramic is placed on a stable but somewhat soft surface, like a piece of MDF with several layers of paper towels, with the front facing down.

Shapes

Ceramic is normally an easy material to work with, and very complex shapes can be achieved without making use of any special process.

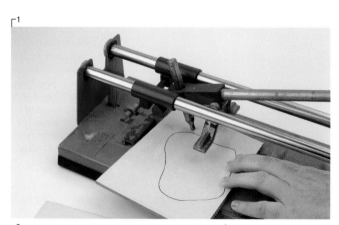

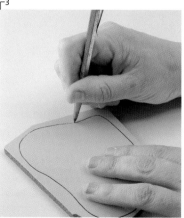

1. After the shape is marked on the ceramic with a permanent marker, the outside of the tile is removed with the tile cutter.

2. The cuts are made as close as possible to the desired shape, while leaving some margin around the line.

3. The line is traced with the scoring stylus. It should be held perpendicular to the surface of the tile and pressure applied while making the line. The point of the stylus marks the tile much like the cutting wheel.

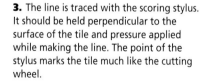

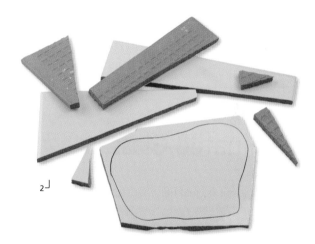

4. The excess tile is broken off with the pliers. Their jaws should be aligned with the outside of the scored line and squeezed firmly until the ceramic is cut.

5. Finally, the sides are polished. They are rubbed with a dressing stone, smoothing the outside of the piece a little until achieving the desired shape.

Making Pieces in the Studio

Creating mosaics is not just a matter of assembling the work based on a design by gluing commercial pieces to the support. The art of the mosaic, far from being a limited discipline, allows for the use of pieces made with innovative materials and those made in the studio. The possibility of creating your own pieces is assuredly one of the most creative aspects of this art and opens up a wide field of experimentation.

Laminated Glass

Laminating, that is, making a structure composed of two laminations or sheets of glass, allows us to create pieces with inclusions. Inclusion is a term that in crystallography designates a substance that is caught in the crystal at the moment it crystallized. By extension, it designates the technique consisting of laminating a material between two sheets of glass—it is possible to make our own pieces by placing a thin layer of material between two sheets of glass and using a strong two-part transparent adhesive (epoxy resin and hardener) that will ensure the solidity of the object.

Pigment and Paint Inclusions

These inclusions, in reality, consist of coloring the adhesive (a transparent compound), with the addition of pigments or paint. It is very important to follow the manufacturer's recommendations on the container relating to safety, and to the working and drying times.

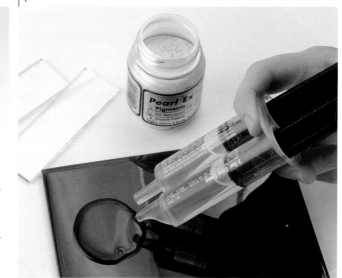

1. To make colored pieces, powdered pigments can be used. A small amount of two-part adhesive (whatever you think necessary based on the dimensions of the glass) is applied on an impermeable surface, in this case, a glazed tile.

2. A small amount of powdered pigment is added and mixed with a plastic stick to make a smooth paste.

3. The adhesive is applied to one of the glass pieces with the plastic stick, as seen in the photograph, without getting too close to the edges, because when the other piece of glass is pressed into place on top, the glue will flow and cover the whole space.

4. The second piece of glass is placed over the adhesive so that both pieces are perfectly aligned. Something heavy is placed on the glass (in this case, bolts) and left to dry according to the manufacturer's instructions.

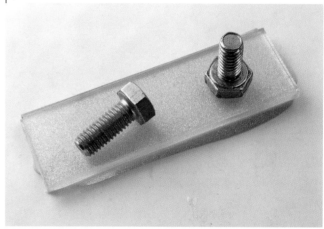

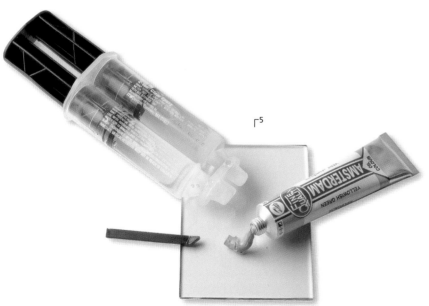

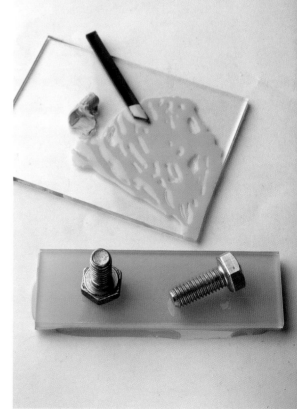

5. The adhesive can also be colored by adding oil paint. Follow the previous instructions, incorporating a small amount of paint in the adhesive and applying the mixture to one of the glass pieces.

6. Here you also must put weight on the piece and allow it to dry. Any extra adhesive is removed with a knife after it is dry.

Metal and Paper Inclusions

The technique of making metal and paper inclusions does not differ in essence from the previous technique.

Inclusions created with metals can be spectacular. Very thin sheets or leaves can be used whole with the adhesive to create smooth or fragmented pieces with a speckled look. It is also possible to mix fragments of different metals to make speckled pieces that combine different colors and tonalities.

Using regular paper (magazines or newspapers, for example) as well as tracing paper (photocopied or drawn on) opens a wide range of possibilities. It is also worth pointing out the different solutions resulting from combining these materials with colored glass as a base. Following are some examples of this:

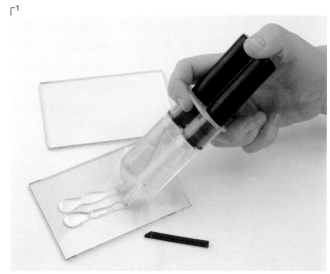

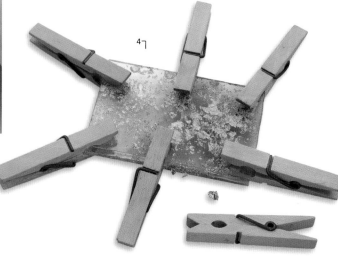

1 and 2. A small amount of adhesive is applied to the lower piece of glass. It is stirred with a plastic stick to make a smooth mixture.

3. Broken-up metal leaf (in this case, gold leaf) is sprinkled on the adhesive until the surface is completely covered.

4. The other piece of glass is placed on the adhesive with both sheets perfectly aligned. Since we are dealing with a large piece, we ensure a good bond by attaching wooden clothespins around the edges. The clothespins apply even pressure all around the piece, helping distribute the adhesive with the inclusions and making a good lamination when it has dried.

Inclusions can also be made with paper (here, newspaper). Adhesive is applied to both pieces of glass, and then the pieces of finely cut-up paper are added. They are combined and clothespins attached (as in the previous example).

1. In this case, a photocopy is used, made on tracing paper, with a design from a clip art book.

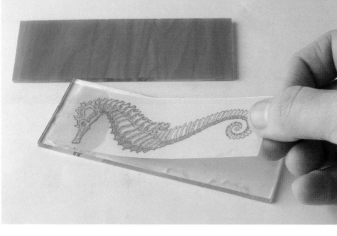

2. The two-part adhesive is applied on both sheets of glass, and then the paper is added. One end should be placed first, then the rest centered and slowly lowered onto the adhesive, avoiding the formation of bubbles underneath. The paper should be somewhat smaller than the piece so the glass will adhere correctly. These pieces cannot be cut and are used whole in the creation of a mosaic.

Inclusions open a wide range of chromatic and formal possibilities. The pieces can be cut (see "Cutting Glass") to create small tiles.

Polymer Clay Tiles

The use of new materials, among them polymer clay, opens new possibilities for creating pieces for mosaics. These can be used to make forms with volume as well as flat pieces. Polymer clay is worked the same way as any modeling clay and can be baked in a normal oven at about 250ºF (130ºC) for 15 minutes, with the pieces arranged on a nonporous surface. The temperature and the time vary according to manufacturer, so it is important to follow the instructions. After they have been baked and then cooled, they can be polished, sanded, drilled, filed, cut, and even painted with water-based acrylic paints.

Polymer clay allows tiles to be made quickly and easily by cutting them right off the block. Then they must be baked in an oven.

Painted Glass

Another option for making pieces in the studio is painting on glass. A special paint is applied directly to the piece of glass. After it is completely dry, the glass is cut according to our requirements (following the process described in the chapter "Cutting Glass"). It should be pointed out that the painted side of the pieces should be in contact with the adhesive in the process of making the mosaic, since the paint is not highly durable and could become damaged with constant use or by regular cleaning.

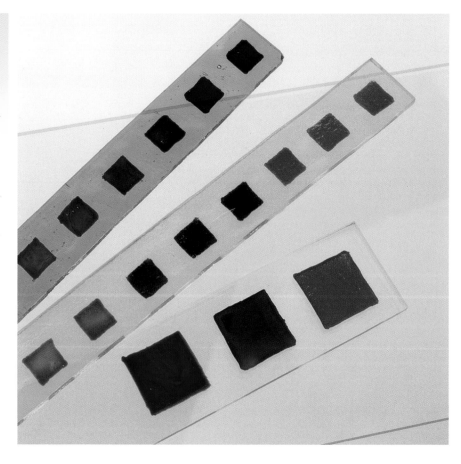

An example of various pieces of glass before they are cut into tiles. Notice the possibilities offered by the different-colored glass—in this case, the three pieces have been painted with three similar colors (red, blue, and purple), which combine with the color of the glass to create different tones.

Acid-Etched Glass

Acid cream lets us decorate the surface of the glass and achieve results in the studio that are similar to commercially done acid-etched work, without the risks that entails. It is used to shade the surface of the glass, creating contrasts with the transparent and shiny parts of the piece. To do this you need to use reserves, which means protecting the surface of the glass with some technique that keeps the cream from coming into contact with it. Reserves can be made with different materials, among them adhesive plastic contact paper, white glue, latex, and paper and plastic adhesive tape, depending on the effect you wish to achieve.

When using the cream it is necessary to have a durable brush, protective gloves if your hands will be coming into contact with the product, and it must be applied in a well-ventilated place. It is very important to always follow the manufacturer's instructions written on the container, to clean up any leftover cream with paper towels, which should be disposed of immediately, and to clean the glass with lots of running water.

⌐¹

1. In this case, the reserve is made with plastic contact paper. The selected design is drawn on the plastic with a permanent marker.

⌐²

2. The shape is cut out with a very sharp craft knife. The protective backing is removed and the plastic is centered and attached to the glass.

3. A generous amount of acid cream is applied to the glass. After the amount of time suggested by the manufacturer has passed (in our case, five minutes), it is removed with a paper towel that is then disposed of. The glass is washed with a large amount of water and the plastic is peeled off.

4⌐
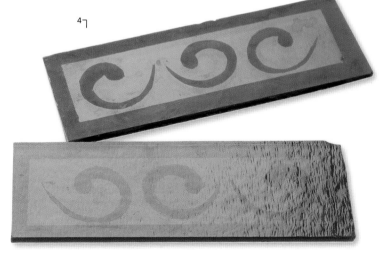

⌐³

4. The pieces created with acid cream have the same characteristics as glass and can be placed with the etched side up or down in the mosaic.

Pieces with Volume

Direct modeling is another technique for creating pieces in the studio. This system is an easy way to make three-dimensional pieces. You do not need a great amount of skill or knowledge to model the clay since there are patterns to make it easier. Modeling clay similar to that used for making ceramics, but that does not need to be fired, simplifies the work and allows a wide range of possibilities of form.

It is very important to follow the manufacturer's instructions regarding working and drying times, and the conditions required for conserving the clay.

1. A starfish is chosen as the design motif. It is drawn on a waterproof work surface, such as a board covered with melamine, with a medium-tip permanent marker.

2. The modeling clay is worked on the board using the drawing as a guide.

3. The final result is a three-dimensional piece that will help add some relief to the mosaic.

Painted Pieces

Painting is a good technique for decorating three-dimensional pieces. It is applied to the dried and carefully sanded clay, and always requires a final coat of varnish.

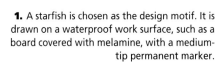

1. After the piece is completely dry, rough edges are removed and the sides are smoothed with fine-grit sandpaper (in this case, 220).

2. The surface is painted, using different tones of yellow, red, and orange acrylic paint. Then it is left to dry.

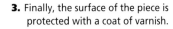

3. Finally, the surface of the piece is protected with a coat of varnish.

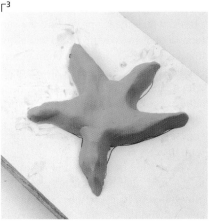

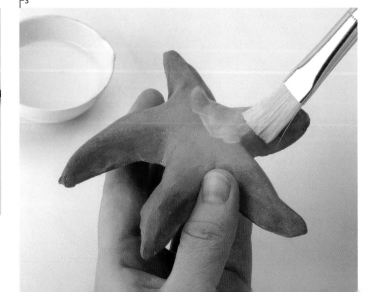

Pieces with Mosaic

One of the possibilities offered by modeling clay is adding pieces to the surface. These can be of the same material, made beforehand and dried, or of ceramic, glass, plastic, etc. They are embedded in the clay before it has begun to dry.

1. We have chosen to use glass in two amber tones to make this mosaic. Several wavy strips are made, and then cut into small tile shapes with cutting pliers.

2. The tiles are inserted into the surface of the star. They should all be perfectly level with the surface of the piece.

3. Here is the piece after it has dried. The result is decorated with mosaics and can become part of a larger work made using the same technique.

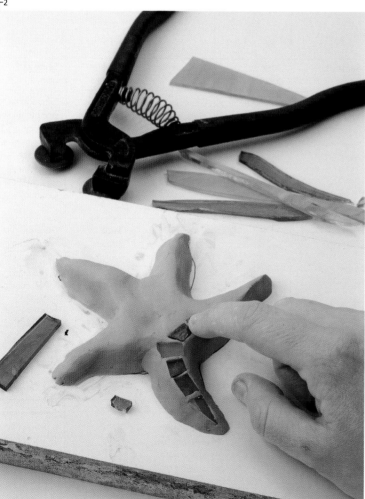

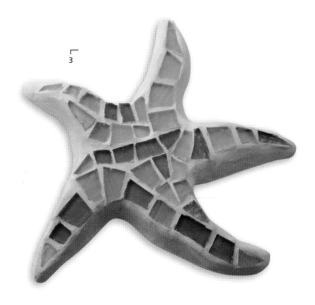

CHART

64

INTERIOR Placement Systems

	WALLS							
	Damp Areas			Dry Areas			Damp Areas	
	Support		Materials	Support		Materials	Support	Materials
	Floor Tiles	Cement, concrete, and brick walls		Plaster and gypsum panel walls	Cement, concrete, and brick walls		Cement surfaces	
	Adhesives			Adhesives			Adhesive	
DIRECT	Adhesive cement with prior surface preparation with an appropriate product, silicone	Adhesive cement, silicone	Glazed tile, glass tile, glass, shells, enamel tile, stoneware (with a protective finish)	Adhesive cement for plaster or adhesive cement over a surface previously prepared with a solution of 1 part PVA in 1 part water, (1:1) silicone	Adhesive cement, silicone	Glazed and unglazed tile, terra-cotta, glass tile, glass, shells, enamel tiles, stoneware, clay pieces	Adhesive cement, silicone	Durable glazed tile, stoneware (in some cases a protective finish wil be required), glass pieces in low-traffic areas
DIRECT WITH VOLUME	Same as above	Same as above	Same as above	Same as above	Same as above	Same as above	Same as above	Same as above
INDIRECT	Same as above	Same as above	Glass tile, glass, enamel tile, stoneware	Same as above	Adhesive cement or mortar	Glass tile, glass, enamel tile, stoneware, terra-cotta	Adhesive cement or mortar	Terra-cotta and stoneware (in some cases, a protective finish is required), glass pieces in low-traffic areas
INDIRECT FOR PAVERS	—	—	—	—	—	—	Same as above	Durable glazed tile, stoneware, glass pieces in low-traffic areas. A protective finish will be required.
DOUBLE INDIRECT	Same as above	Same as above	Glazed tile, glass tile, glass, shells, enamel tile, stoneware (with a protective finish)	Same as above	Adhesive cement or mortar	Glazed and unglazed tile, terra-cotta, glass tile, glass, shells, enamel tiles, stoneware, clay pieces	Same as above	Durable glazed tile, terra-cotta and stoneware (in some cases, a protective finish will be required), glass pieces in low-traffic areas

FLOORS			OBJECTS, FURNITURE, AND PANELS						
Dry Areas									
Support	**Support**		**Support**		**Support**		**Support**		
Cement surfaces	Wood (solid, plywood, and MDF)	**Materials**	Wood panels (solid, MDF, and plywood), wood furniture surfaces and tops	**Materials**	Glass	**Materials**	Terra-cotta, formica, and PVC	**Materials**	
Adhesive			**Adhesive**		**Adhesive**		**Adhesive**		
Adhesive cement, silicone	Adhesive cement with latex, silicone	Durable glazed and unglazed tile, terra-cotta, stoneware, glass pieces in low-traffic areas	Adhesive cement with latex, silicone	Glazed and unglazed tile, terra-cotta, glass tile, glass, shells, enamel tile, stoneware, clay pieces, etc.	Transparent silicone for glass	Glass is the most-used material since it lets light through, but other lightweight materials such as tile, glass tile, enamel tile, or pieces of clay can be used to create opaque areas	Adhesive cement, silicone	Glazed and unglazed tile, terra-cotta, glass tile, glass, shells, enamel tile, stoneware, clay pieces, etc.	
Same as above	Same as above	Same as above	Same as above	Same as above	Same as above	Same as above	Same as above	Same as above	
Adhesive cement or mortar	Same as above	Terra-cotta and stoneware, glass pieces in low-traffic areas	Same as above	Terra-cotta, glass tile, glass, enamel tile, stoneware	—	—	Same as above	Same as above	
Same as above	Same as above	Terra-cotta and stoneware, glass pieces in low-traffic areas	—	—	—	—	—	—	
Same as above	Same as above	Durable glazed and unglazed tile, terra-cotta, stoneware, glass pieces in low-traffic areas	Same as above	Glazed and unglazed tile, terra-cotta, glass tile, glass, shells, enamel tile, stoneware, clay pieces, etc.	—	—	Same as above	Same as above	

CHART

66

EXTERIOR Placement Systems

	WALLS		FLOORS		FOUNTAINS, PONDS, POOLS	
	Support Cement, concrete, fiber cement, and brick / **Adhesive**	**Materials**	**Support** Cement surfaces / **Adhesive**	**Materials**	**Support** Cement and concrete surfaces and walls / **Adhesive**	**Materials**
DIRECT	Adhesive cement (depending on the local climate, freeze-proof adhesive cement may be necessary), silicone	Glazed tile, glass tile, glass, enamel tile, stoneware	Adhesive cement (depending on the local climate, freeze-proof adhesive cement may be necessary), silicone	Durable glazed tile, stoneware (in some cases, a protective finish is required), glass pieces in low-traffic areas	Adhesive cement (depending on the local climate, freeze-proof adhesive cement may be necessary), silicone	Durable glazed tile, glass tile, glass, some stoneware, shells (with a protective finish)
DIRECT WITH VOLUME	Same as above	Same as above	—	—	Same as above	Same as above
INDIRECT	Same as above	Glass tile, glass, enamel tile, stoneware	Adhesive cement or mortar (depending on the local climate, freeze-proof adhesive cement may be necessary)	Stoneware (in certain cases, a protective finish must be applied), glass pieces in low-traffic areas	Same as above	Glass tile, glass, some stoneware (with a protective finish)
INDIRECT FOR PAVERS	—	—	Same as above	Same as above	—	—
DOUBLE INDIRECT	Same as above	Glazed tile, glass tile, glass, enamel tile, stoneware	Same as above	Durable glazed tile, stoneware (in some cases, a protective finish is required), glass pieces in low-traffic areas	Same as above	Durable glazed tile, glass tile, glass, some stoneware, shells (with a protective finish

TABLE TOPS AND PANELS				CONTAINERS AND GARDEN ELEMENTS	
Support / **Adhesives** Fiber cement surfaces and exterior treated wood	**Materials**	**Support** / **Adhesives** Terra-cotta	**Materials**	**Support** / **Adhesives** PVC surfaces	**Materials**
Adhesive cement (depending on the local climate, freeze-proof adhesive cement may be required), or vinyl acetate adhesive (EVA), silicone	Glazed tile, glass tile, glass, some stoneware	Adhesive cement (depending on the local climate, freeze-proof adhesive cement may be required), silicone on a surface previously prepared with vinyl acetate adhesive (EVA), silicone	Glazed tile, glass tile, glass, enamel tile, stoneware, shells	Silicone, two-part epoxy resin	Glazed tile, glass tile, glass, enamel tile, stoneware, shells
Same as above	Same as above	Same as above	Same as above	Same as above	Same as above
Same as above	Glass tile, glass, some stoneware	Same as above	Glass tile, glass, enamel tile, stoneware	Same as above	Glass tile, glass, enamel tile, stoneware
—	—	—	—	—	—
Same as above	Glazed tile, glass tile, glass, enamel tile, some stoneware, shells	Same as above	Glazed tile, glass tile, glass, enamel tile, stoneware, shells	Same as above	Glazed tile, glass tile, glass, enamel tile, stoneware, shells

Placement Techniques

The art of mosaics is based on creating works by assembling different pieces on a support. This discipline, which seems simple, entails a series of techniques that are very different from each other and that are used according to each case, based on the support, the nature of the pieces, and the environment in which the mosaic will be placed after it is finished. Generally speaking, each mosaic will be made using the technique that is appropriate for it, although in some cases, it will be necessary to combine various techniques to create the work of art.

Direct Placement

This is the easiest technique for assembling a mosaic and therefore the best one to begin with. It consists of gluing the pieces directly to the support with adhesive or mortar. This system allows us to always be in control of each step and its result, making fast and efficient progress. It always requires a preliminary design on the support, which will serve as a guiding pattern while placing and gluing the pieces. This technique does not render even surfaces, unless similar pieces of different colors are used, but it works well for works of either small or large format.

Here we choose a very simple design as an example so only the main motif is drawn. In more complicated or larger work it is a good idea to apply the complete design on the support.

1. The design is traced on the support. In this case, the central design of the composition, a fish, is drawn on paper, then it is traced onto the support (plywood) using graphite paper.

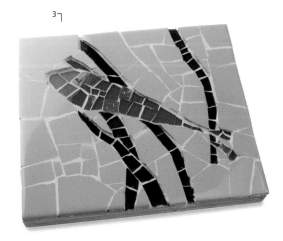

2. The previously cut or broken pieces are applied directly to the wood with white PVA glue, following the design.

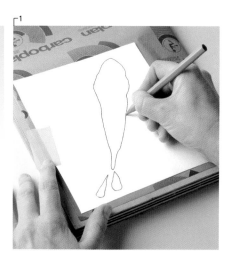

3. Here is the finished mosaic, with the glue completely dry and finished with white grout. Red glass and enamel (*smalti*) tiles were used to make the fish, the seaweed was done with green glass, and the background with glazed blue tiles. Notice that pieces of tile with finished rounded edges were placed on the four sides of the mosaic.

Direct Placement on a Volume

Any support with volume or three dimensions can be covered using mosaic techniques. Direct placement on a volume is no different, in essence, from working on a flat surface, although in this case, the adhesive cement or mortar that is used should allow a good immediate bond to keep the pieces from moving after they have been attached to the support.

1. In the following example a transparent glass is decorated with different-colored glass (cathedral green and iridescent white) in vertical strips and green squares, turning it into a candleholder.

2. The height and perimeter of the support are measured and the dimensions (height and width) are established for the glass strips, which will alternate in color. The glass is cut, first scoring the lines with the glass cutter, using graph paper as a pattern. Pliers are used to separate the pieces.

3. The strips are glued in a vertical pattern, alternating the colors and aligning the strips with the base of the support. A square glass tile is glued in the open space above each strip. Notice that a heavy tool is used to hold the glass steady while working.

4. Finally, the silicone is left to dry according to the manufacturers' recommendations.

5. The joints are filled using a paint scraper, with grout that has been colored (see "Preparations and Finishes") to combine with the tones of the mosaic.

6. Before it is completely dry, the grout that is on the pieces is removed with a paper towel. It is left to dry for at least 30 minutes.

7. The top part of the mosaic is leveled and lightly sanded with a 220-grit paper in case there are any traces of grout left.

8. Here is the finished piece.

Indirect Placement

This placement system can be applied only by using pieces with both sides of the same color, for example, glass, enamel tiles, and glass tiles. It is not appropriate for ceramic pieces with only one decorated side. The technique consists of creating the mosaic using a temporary support (usually brown wrapping paper), gluing the pieces to it and then attaching it to the permanent support, then removing the paper that covers it. The most complicated part is that the mosaic is created backward from the way it will be when in place; the design on the paper will be the opposite of the final one, in other words, it will be a mirror image of the original.

This system allows us to appreciate the progress of the work and to know how the final composition of the mosaic will look. At the same time, it will permit us to make changes and variations while working. Its greatest advantage resides in the fact that it is possible to create most of the work, the actual assembly of the mosaic, in the studio and later transport it to the final location. In the following example we show how to create a mosaic tile.

1. The design is created based on the selected pieces (round glass pieces, glass tiles, and unglazed ceramic squares); the colors and central motif are selected: the round pieces. A temporary support of brown wrapping paper with lines marking the outside of the tile has been previously made.

2. The design is drawn on the paper with a pencil and redrawn with a marker. The squares are cut to the desired size and glued to the support with methylcellulose adhesive. They should be glued face down, that is, the upper side that will be visible when the mosaic is finished is in contact with the paper.

3. This is the finished composition. The circular pieces will be glued using the direct placement method, so they will not be assembled at this time, but make sure that they will fit into the free spaces. If any changes or adjustments are required, they will be done at this stage.

4. The extra paper is cut off to make it easier to place on the final support.

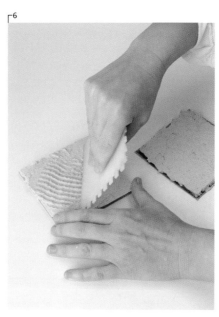

5. A layer of adhesive cement is applied to the permanent support (an unglazed ceramic tile). Then it is applied to the mosaic with a scraper.

6. The adhesive cement on the support is scraped with a notched trowel to improve the adhesion of the two pieces.

7. Then the mosaic is carefully placed on the support and light pressure is applied.

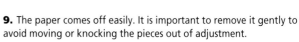

8. The paper is dampened with a wet sponge while the cement is still fresh.

9. The paper comes off easily. It is important to remove it gently to avoid moving or knocking the pieces out of adjustment.

10. Now the circular pieces are put in place. Some of the cement is removed with a wooden spatula, then the pieces are put into place with a light pressure. It is still possible to make small adjustments in the location of the pieces and tiles.

11. Traces of adhesive cement that is in the joints between the pieces are removed before it is completely dry. In the areas where the separation between the pieces is wider, the cement is removed with an awl.

12. In very narrow separations, thin picks are used to extract the cement. Then it is left to dry according to the manufacturer's recommendations.

13. Finally, white grout is added, taking care to fill all the joints. It is left to dry for 30 minutes and then cleaned.

14. Appearance of the mosaic after the job is finished.

Indirect for Pavers

Creating paving tiles with mosaic requires a special technique. This consists of making a mosaic using the indirect system and then placing it inside a frame that acts as a mold with walls for the mortar. A first layer is applied, then a metal screen is placed on it to strengthen the base of the mosaic, after which the final layer of mortar is added. Pieces made using this technique are heavy and very durable; they are ideal for use outdoors.

1. The design is drawn on the paper. Then the materials and pieces for making the mosaic are selected, in this case, stones, white marble, and unglazed tile.

2. The outside border is made first. Some marble squares are cut with a cold chisel then glued to the paper with methylcellulose adhesive.

3. The curving band, the central stone, and the background are glued in. Pliers are used to break up the ceramic tile. As in the previous project, all the pieces and tiles are glued in upside down, so the side that will be visible when the mosaic is finished is in contact with the paper.

4. When the adhesive has dried, a generous amount of colored grout is applied, and spread with a trowel, making sure that it penetrates all the spaces well. It is then left to dry for 30 minutes.

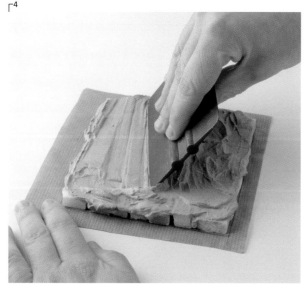

5. A wood frame is made with dimensions similar to those of the mosaic by attaching four pieces of wood with screws. A layer of petroleum jelly is applied to the wood as a release agent so the mortar will not adhere to it.

6. The mosaic is placed on a waterproof surface and inside the frame with the paper-covered surface face down. A layer of mortar is applied and smoothed well.

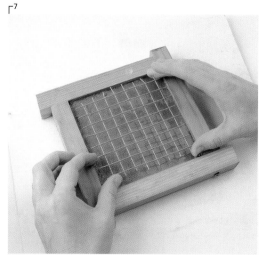

7. The metal screen, cut to fit, is placed on the layer of mortar.

8. This is covered with a second layer of mortar, smoothed, and made level with the wood frame. The work surface is struck several times to eliminate any possible air bubbles in the mortar. They will work their way up and disappear.

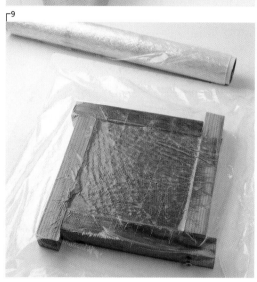

9. The surface is covered with plastic to help the mortar cure. It is left to dry for three days.

10. The frame is taken apart. The paper that covers the surface of the mosaic is dampened with a wet sponge and removed. Notice that some spaces have not been filled with the mortar.

11. Mortar is applied to cover all the joints and to level the surface, and is left to dry for 30 minutes. It is then cleaned with a rag, and any grout remaining on the tiles and in the nooks and crannies is scraped with a metal spatula until they are completely removed.

Double Indirect

This technique is appropriate for making mosaics with pieces that do not have the same color on both sides, where the front is different from the back as on glazed tiles. This placement method represents an innovation in the creation of mosaic work, making the process easier when these materials are used. It also allows us to combine other materials along with tiles in the same mosaic.

The technique consists of gluing the pieces to a sheet of acetate following the design, that is, just as they will be arranged in the final mosaic with the top surfaces up. Next, a sheet of wrapping paper is glued over them, the composition is turned upside down, and the acetate is removed. Finally, the mosaic is placed on the mortar and the pieces are leveled.

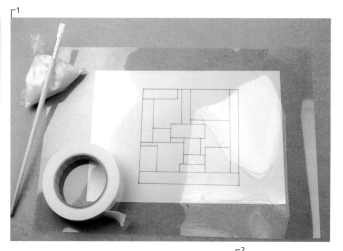

1. The design is placed on the work surface and covered with a sheet of acetate, attaching the corners to the surface with masking tape.

2. After the pieces (glazed tile, unglazed tile, glass, and gold enamel or *smalti*) have been cut to size, they are glued to the acetate with methylcellulose adhesive. Notice that they are arranged exactly as they will appear when the mosaic is finished.

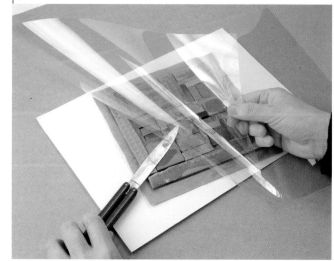

3. Wrapping paper is cut slightly larger than the mosaic and a generous amount of methylcellulose adhesive is applied to one side. The side with the glue is placed over the mosaic and light pressure is applied. Then it is left to dry.

4. The mosaic is turned over very carefully so that the acetate sheet is now on top.

5. The acetate is easily removed by sliding the blade of a knife or spatula under it while pulling it back.

6. A mold is made with wood using masking tape, and the support and a layer of mortar are then put inside of it.

7. After carefully aligning the sides of the mosaic with those of the mold, it is placed on the mortar as if it were the page of a book.

8. Since the pieces are of a different thickness, it is necessary to level the surface of the mosaic. A wood panel is placed on the surface and struck with a hammer.

9. The mortar is allowed to dry. The paper is dampened with a wet sponge and pulled off. Then the frame is taken apart.

10. Here is the mosaic after the grout was applied.

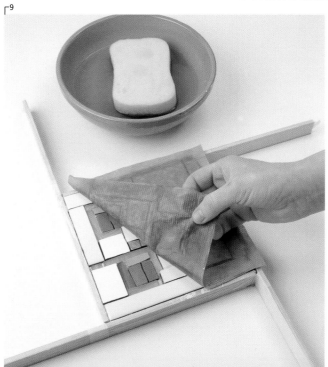

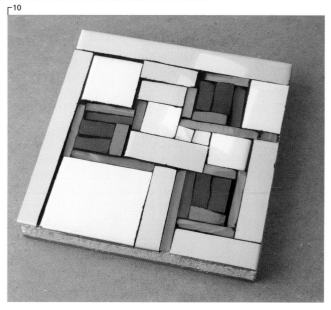

Mixtures and Finishes

Different approaches can be used during the various stages in the creation of a mosaic. Thus, the creative possibilities (without taking into account the design) do not end with the use of materials and the creation of pieces or with the different placement techniques. The mixtures permit us to adjust the mortar and vary the color of the grout according to the characteristics of the work. The finishes give it its final look and help preserve it.

Mixtures

Although it is possible to purchase a great variety of mortars and grouts that are ready to use, the mixtures can also be made in the studio. Mixing these products is not at all difficult, nor does it require special knowledge, and it helps reduce the cost of the project.

There are a large number of mortar recipes, some of which are shown here.

SOME MORTAR RECIPES	
Mortar	1 part white and/or portland cement + 3 parts sand (1 volume of white and/or portland cement + 3 volumes of sand)
Mortar with lime	1 part white and/or portland cement + 3 parts sand + 1/2 part lime (1 volume of white and/or portland cement + 3 volumes of sand; 1/2 volume of lime)
Mortar with marble	1 part white cement + 3 parts marble dust (1 volume of white cement + 3 volumes of marble dust)

Mortar with Latex

Mortar with latex is appropriate for gluing and holding mosaic pieces to previously prepared wood supports. This mixture is commercially available, although mixing it is very easy and can be done in the studio. It is made by adding one-half volume of latex to one volume of previously mixed commercial mortar.

1. Commercial mortar, water, and latex are required to prepare the mixture.

2. The mortar is prepared by adding water according to the manufacturer's instructions, and is mixed until a thick paste is created. Next, the half-volume of latex is added and stirred until thoroughly mixed.

Grout with Pigments

The use of powdered pigments of a single color or mixed colors allows us to create an unlimited number of mixtures. The mixing is always done dry, first adding the grout powder to the pigments, and then the water. The color of the first mixture (dry) is the way the grout will look when it has dried in the mosaic. This will be the guide for establishing the quantity and combinations of pigments, if any.

1. In this example we see how an emerald green grout is mixed. Blue and green powdered pigments are used.

2. The pigments are added to the grout powder and stirred until completely mixed.

3 and 4. The correct amount of water is added (according to the manufacturer's instructions) and stirred until an evenly colored mixture is created. Notice the color of the mixture after the water is added.

Tinted Grout

This mixture is done after the grout has been prepared, adding the color directly to the preparation. The final color of the mixture will be that of the tint, but after it has been added to the mosaic and dried, the color will be less saturated. This and the previous version can be used equally well, no matter what the characteristics of the mosaic are.

1. The grout can be colored using universal tint made for paint.

2. First, the grout is prepared by adding water according to the manufacturer's instructions until a paste is formed.

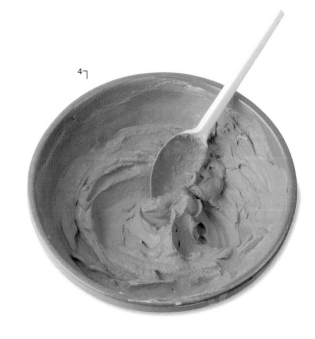

3. Next, the tint is added and stirred until the color is even.

4. The final color of the grout is similar to that of the tint.

Finishes

Finishes are applied to the mosaic when the work is completed. Changing the color of the grout and protecting the surface of the work highlights the finished mosaic.

Painting the Joints

This finishing technique is based on the properties of the grout. After it is dry, it is porous and able to absorb a certain amount of paint and integrate it into the joints so that it forms part of its surface layer. The joints are colored with a water-based paint, which is why this technique is recommended only for mosaics that are indoors and not subject to wear and tear, such as wall pieces and other decorative applications.

1. A water-based color is used for painting the joints, in this case, watercolor. The paint is applied directly to the grout.

2. Some of the seams have been painted; notice the difference between them and those with the original color.

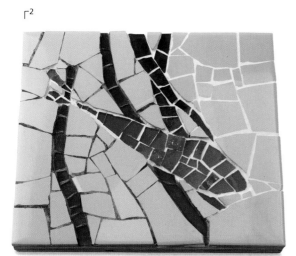

3. The paint is allowed to dry. The grout in the figure of the fish is not painted.

4. The excess paint on the surface of the tiles is removed by lightly rubbing them with a damp paper towel.

5. A pair of tweezers holding a damp cotton ball is used to eliminate traces of paint in small areas and areas that are lower than the surrounding pieces.

6. Here is the mosaic with the painted grout.

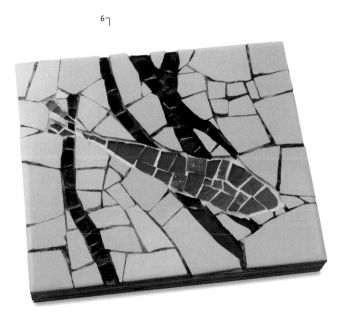

Waxing

Wax is a finish that helps protect the surface of the mosaic, although it is sensitive to excess humidity (it turns white) and offers little protection against scratches. However, it is the most appropriate finish for creating patinas on mosaics with colored wax. It is applied with a cotton rag, and after drying, it is polished by buffing with a clean cotton rag.

The wax is applied with a cotton rag, spreading it evenly over the surface of the mosaic.

¹

Varnishing

Varnish efficiently protects any mosaic, whether outdoors or indoors. It is more durable than wax and some special varnishes (resistant to sunlight and other climatic agents, resistant to mold, and durable for pavers and floors, etc.) even help preserve mosaics.

2

1. Varnish is applied to the mosaic with a brush to form a uniform coat.

2. It offers a more durable finish than wax.

4

Projects

This chapter presents the step-by-step
development of ten mosaic projects. The entire
creative process is explained in full detail, from the original
design to the final placement of the mosaic in its final location. Some
projects have been designed for outdoors and others for indoors, however,
certain mosaics can be used indiscriminately. In all of the cases, innovative
solutions and new materials and supports are introduced, created, as far as
technique is concerned, with methods that complement what has been
explained in the previous chapter. Also shown are specific systems
for achieving particular solutions, such as integrating mosaic into
architecture. These projects should be viewed only as a
starting point where artists can find multiple resources—
ideas, working methods and systems—as well as
solutions for developing their own works of art.

Decorating with Mosaics

Mosaic is an art form that is based on the creation of works through the incorporation of pieces or parts on a support, which can be partially or completely covered. Traditionally, it has been considered an artistic form similar to painting, although more durable, used to decorate surfaces with two-dimensional representations derived from pictorial models. However, the logical evolution of this art and its recent reevaluation as a decorative form has revealed new possibilities that have established a language of its own.

Creating the Setting with Mosaic

Mosaic is a very versatile art form, which can be incorporated into any setting. After overcoming the two-dimensional limitation, mosaic has adapted solutions from three-dimensional artistic forms, adopting the language of volume and texture along with color and form. To this, we add the wide range of possibilities offered by new materials when it comes to parts and supports, as well as modern adhesives. Mosaic art can form part of any space, by completely covering any hard surface or just being an integral part of it, without any other limitations than those defined by the inherent characteristics, resistance, weight, and durability of the materials involved.

Private residence in Sant Joan de les Abadesses, Spain. Mosaic created by Lívia Garreta in 1999. Interior design by Sebastià Vilarasau.

This is not just an art limited to floor and wall decoration, it has extended to every discipline of decoration, either public or private. In the public setting, mosaics constitute a very interesting resource for urban use, giving it character by highlighting or integrating the surfaces into the overall project, coupling the practical aspect with the esthetic and representational. In private spaces, interior or exterior, this decorative alternative is gaining followers, and is used as much for creating new works as for remodeling. It is possible to integrate new creations (full-scale or details) on floors, walls, and surfaces, and decorative elements as well, for example, framed panels, screens, sculptures, stained glass. Mosaics can also be used to refurbish old furniture or construction features to give them a new decorative look or use.

Wall mirror with a frame made also of mirror mosaic. Damien Morrison, 2002.

Salamander. Decorative detail integrated into the tiled wall of a bathroom in a private residence in Barcelona, Spain. Mosaic and glasswork by Philippa Beveridge, 1998,

Backsplash

This project illustrates the process for making a backsplash. The mosaic is created with the direct method using natural elements (sea-shells) and pieces made in the studio with painted and varnished modeling clay. Their combination and arrangement on the support defines the overall composition, which is complemented with ceramic tiles and glass tiles. To create the backsplash itself, a gypsum panel is used as support, which is waterproofed after the mosaic is finished and the joints grouted. The result is a very practical and decorative piece, which gives the bathroom a personal touch and protects the wall surface from the humidity and splashing.

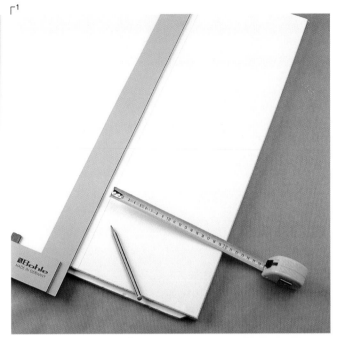

1. A 3/4-inch (2-cm)-thick panel of laminated plaster is used to create this backsplash. The length and width of the mosaic are marked with a pencil, in this case 7 1/2 by 20 inches (19 x 50 cm).

2. The piece is cut out with a saw fitted with a special blade for cutting gypsum board.

3. The sides are sanded and leveled with a fine-grain sandpaper (220 grit) until the edges are perfectly square. The sandpaper is wrapped around a wide piece of wood to ensure an even result.

4. The holes for the screws to attach the backsplash to the wall are made with a drill fitted with a 5/16-inch (8-mm) bit for drilling holes in walls. Two holes are drilled in each corner of the panel, 3/4 inch (2 cm) from the sides.

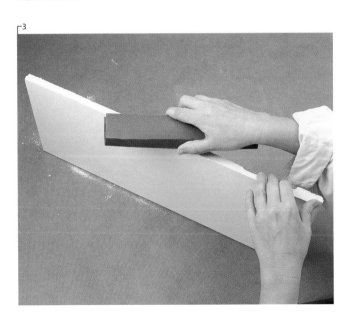

5. Natural materials (seashells) and specially made pieces (starfish made of modeling clay painted and varnished) have been chosen as the main motifs. The ceramic tiles and glass tiles are used for the background and the sides of the composition.

6. The seashells and the starfish are arranged on the plaster panel.

7. The placement of each piece is marked on the panel by tracing its outline with a pencil. The exact placement is indicated with a number or letter written inside of each shape's drawing, and on each corresponding piece. The backs of the starfish are marked with a letter.

8. The seashells are identified by writing a number with a marker on a piece of masking tape that has been attached to them.

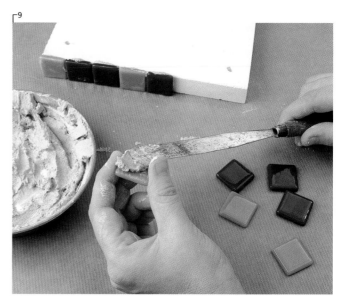

9. First, the glass tiles are placed on the sides of the panel with adhesive cement. The four sides are covered, alternating light blue tiles with dark blue pieces.

10. The insides of the seashells are filled with the same kind of mortar, and they are left to dry. This makes the pieces more resistant, and it also provides a flat surface to make sure that they adhere to the panel properly.

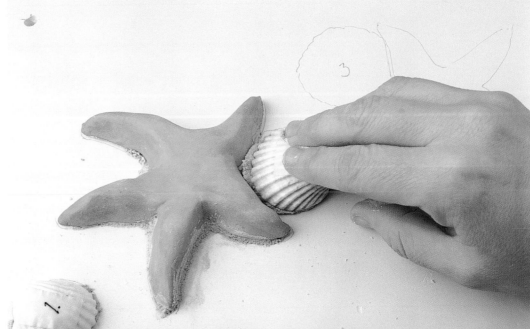

11. The pieces are attached to the panel with mortar according to the placement assigned.

12. After attaching all the pieces that form the central motif, the background pieces, which consist of blue and matte green glazed tiles, are placed. The fragmented pieces are attached to the panel with the mortar, alternating colors.

13. The tile pieces that cover the holes made to attach the panel to the wall will not be added yet. Each piece or set of pieces is marked with a letter, which is written on masking tape and attached to the panel and to each tile fragment.

14. The tile fragments, all with finished edges, are arranged on all four sides of the backsplash.

15. The mosaic after the direct placement of all the pieces. The four tile pieces that will cover the mounting holes have not been added yet.

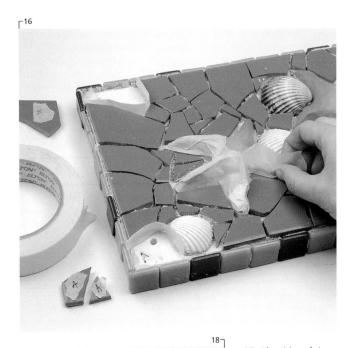

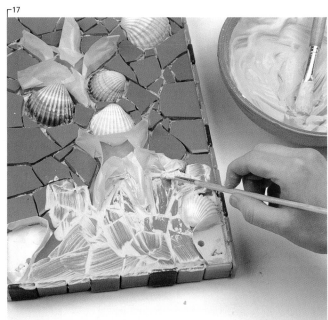

16. The sides of the starfish and the exposed areas are well protected with masking tape.

17. The joints between the pieces are filled with white mildew-resistant grout, and left to dry for a minimum of 30 minutes.

18. The masking tape is removed and the grout is wiped off the tiles with a paper towel.

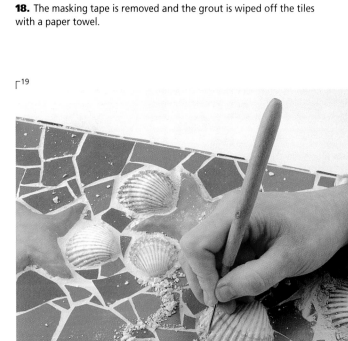

19. An awl is used to remove the grout that may have been deposited on the ridges of the seashells.

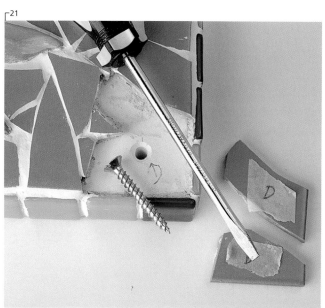

20. The mosaic after the grouting is finished.

21. The backsplash is attached to the wall with long flathead screws. The holes have been countersunk so the screws' heads will be level with the surface. Once they have been screwed in, the tile pieces are placed over them and plastered.

22. View of the backsplash completely finished.

Decorative Wall Detail

One of the many possibilities offered by mosaics is the creation of decorative wall details. The creation of this type of mosaic with a particular variation of the indirect system makes the work easier and the process considerably simplified. It consists of applying the mosaic directly to a temporary support that is later integrated into the wall. This method can be used to create interior or exterior mosaic pieces.

The support (plastic mesh or fiberglass) is placed over the mosaic's pattern, separated from it by a plastic sheet. Then the pieces or tile are placed directly on the mesh. Once the mosaic is dry and finished, the pattern is removed. It is necessary to prepare the wall area beforehand by removing the plaster and paint that cover it. The material used to attach the mosaic (adhesive cement) is very strong and could pull off the wall covering after it sets if it is not in perfect condition. At the same time, the preparation guarantees the proper adhesion of the work to the wall surface.

1. We begin with a motif taken from a book that offers a wide selection of seashells of the world. Once the shape has been chosen, a black and white enlarged photocopy of the motif is made to match the real size of the mosaic (6 x 6 inches) [15 x 15 cm]. This will serve as the model. Another color photocopy is made as well, which will be used as a guide during the entire creative process. Glass tile and stoneware tesserae are the chosen materials.

2. The motif is cut out and attached to the support, a piece of wood with a melamine veneer, with masking tape.

3. It is covered with a layer of plastic film, which is secured to the back of the wood with masking tape.

4. A piece of heavy plastic mesh is cut out, a little larger than the motif itself, and attached to the plastic with tape.

5. Using the original colors as a reference, the tesserra fragments are attached with white PVA glue.

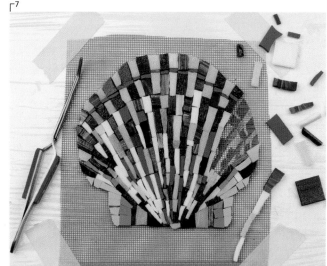

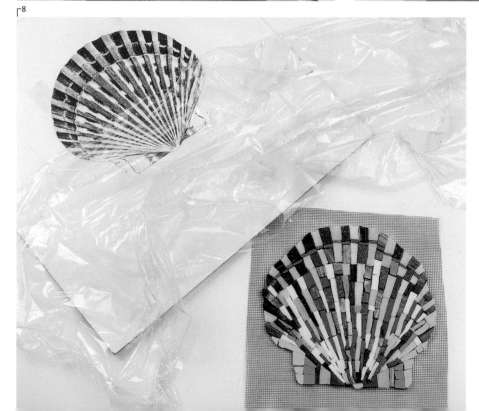

6. The small fragments are arranged and placed with tweezers.

7. Before each row is glued on, it is important to try out different compositions to establish possible color combinations.

8. Once the mosaic is finished, the glue is left to dry for a minimum of 24 hours. Afterward, the mesh is removed from the support.

9. The excess mesh is removed, leaving the support aligned with the edge of the mosaic.

10. Using the mosaic as a guide, the outline is marked on the selected wall. The wall covering (plaster and paint) is removed with a scraper and a hammer until the underlying surface is exposed.

9

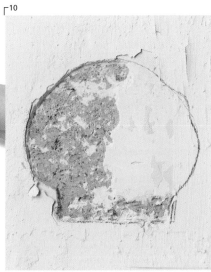

10

11

11. A layer of adhesive cement is applied to make a flat and smooth surface, leaving a difference in the level equal to the mosaic's thickness.

12. The mosaic is placed over the adhesive cement without applying too much pressure.

13. To level the surface of the mosaic, a piece of wood is placed over the mosaic and is tapped with a hammer. The procedure is repeated until the mosaic is fully integrated into the wall.

13

12

14. Now, adhesive cement is used to seal the pieces. A generous amount is spread with a scraper, making sure that it is inserted in the spaces between the tesserae.

15. Before it dries completely, the excess is wiped off with a sponge dampened in water, then it is left to dry.

16. This mosaic decorates an outside column in the porch of a house.

Flowerpot Holder

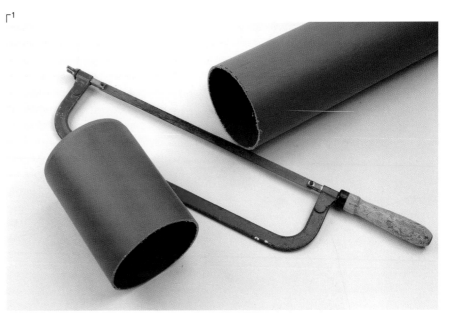

Mosaic art makes it possible to create objects that perfectly combine their practical and decorative aspects. Here, the creation of an outdoor stand, which is used to hold a flowerpot as well as to decorate a corner of the house or garden, is explained step by step. The mosaic is made using the direct placement method over a volume made of polyvinyl chloride tubing normally used in construction, which is very durable and affordable. A detailed presentation of how to make a pattern is shown, which is then transferred to the surface of the volume. This method can be applied to any work by extrapolating it to a project.

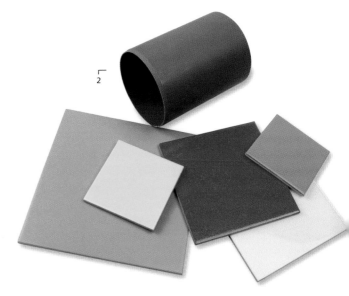

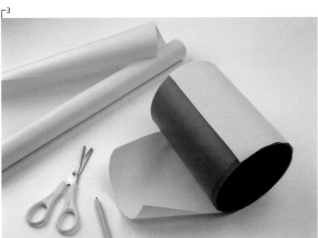

1. The support chosen is a piece of polyvinyl chloride (PVC) tubing, 4 1/2 inches (11 cm) in diameter. A 6-inch (5-cm)-long section is cut out.

2. Yellow, red, orange, and light ocher glazed and unglazed tiles are used.

3. To make a pattern that fits the shape, one of the ends of the paper is taped to the PVC tube. Then, it is wrapped around the cylinder and the paper is cut at the point where both ends meet. The top and bottom parts are trimmed at the ends of the support, and the paper is removed. The final pattern is a rectangle, resulting from the cylindrical shape of the support.

4. A 3-inch (8-cm) pattern shaped like a long leaf is made on a piece of cardboard. This will be the main motif of the composition. A series of shapes are outlined over the support's pattern, arranging them according to the desired effect.

5. The shapes of the leaves are cut out and attached to the tube's pattern with tape. The inside of the cutout shapes are drawn on the support using a permanent marker with a thick tip. The pattern is removed.

6. The result is a design that has been transferred to the support. The tile pieces that will become the background of the composition are cut out, and the color composition is decided by arranging the fragments before they are glued on.

7. The silhouettes of the leaves are drawn by tracing the outlines of the patterns on the tiles with a permanent marker.

8. The tiles are cut out with a tile cutter. The ragged edges are eliminated with tile pliers, resulting in same-sized leaves of different colors.

9. Each leaf is broken into pieces of different sizes with a pair of tile pliers.

10. The fragments are glued onto the PVC support with transparent silicone. First, the pieces that form the lower part of the background are secured, followed by the leaves.

11. The process begins at the bottom of the holder and progresses to the top.

12. The background pieces are arranged as desired, maintaining the color gradation.

13. Finally, the top border made with glazed red ceramic tile is attached. The silicone is left to dry for a minimum of 24 hours.

14. The mosaic is sealed with colored grout.

15. Before the piece dries out completely, any grout that may have been left on the tiles is removed with a paper towel. The grout is left to dry for 30 minutes, then the excess is removed with a wooden spatula.

16. View of the finished holder.

Christmas Ornaments

The mosaic technique, in addition to creating flat surfaces for a wide range of practical solutions, can also be applied to different materials. Therefore, it is possible to use any hard material as a support for mosaics, a factor that opens an almost endless array of possibilities. This project shows how to make decorative objects with a new material, expanded polystyrene (EPS) or Styrofoam, as a support. It also explains in detail how to cut out any shape using patterns to make four Christmas ornaments for indoors with the direct placement system. Novelty materials are used as well to trim the tree. Finally, it also explains how to make an ornament with modeling clay in two steps, by inserting the mosaic pieces into the support.

1. A wreath, a tree, a reindeer, and a star are drawn on a piece of paper.

2. The motifs are transferred onto heavy construction paper, using tracing paper to make the patterns.

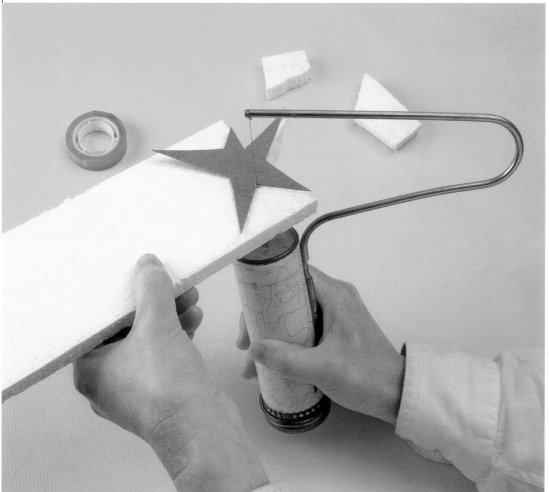

3. The patterns that will serve as guides for making the ornaments are cut out.

4. For the star, the wreath, and the tree the support is created first. The expanded polystyrene is cut out by using the pattern as a guide. The star's pattern is approximately 4 1/2 x 4 1/2 inches (11 x 11 cm) in size.

5. The pattern is placed over a 1/2-inch (1.5-cm)-thick panel of expanded polystyrene and secured to it with a piece of tape placed on the back. The support is cut out with the polystyrene cutter by following the outline.

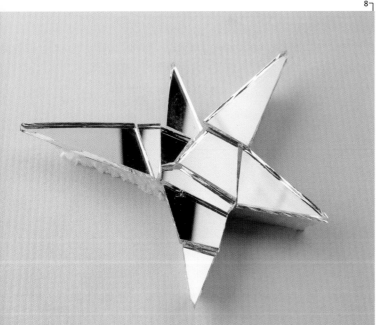

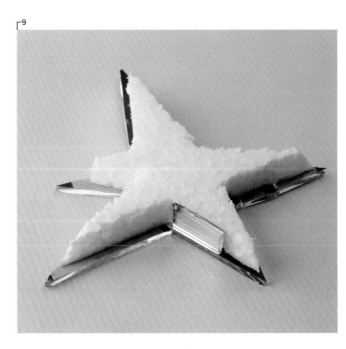

6. A mirror is used to make the star. The cutting line is scored on the mirror and the pieces are separated with pliers.

7. The pieces are attached to the support with a special adhesive for expanded polystyrene. A small amount of the adhesive is placed on the back of the piece and is glued to the support.

8. The assembly of the mosaic begins by covering of one of the faces of the stars.

9. Then the sides are assembled. Rectangular pieces are used, cut to the required size.

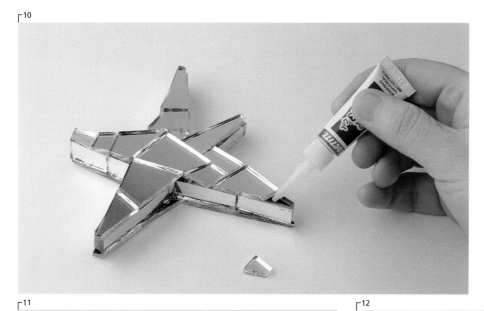

10. The opposite face is covered. When the pieces are very small or are located in difficult parts of the support, cyanoacrilate adhesive is used. It is left to dry for 24 hours.

11. It is sealed with white grout and left to dry for a minimum of 30 minutes.

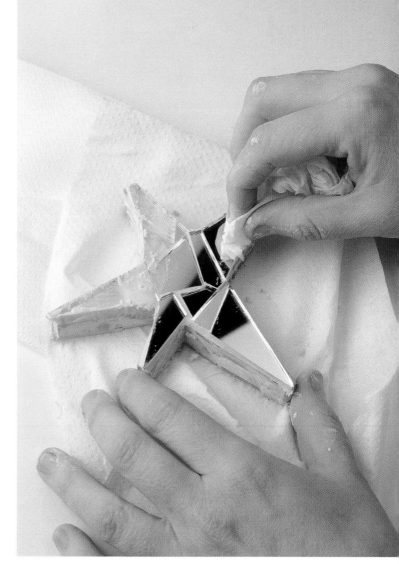

12. The excess grout left on the mirror is wiped off with a paper towel.

13. The same procedure is followed to make the Christmas tree. The support is cut out using a pattern 3 1/2 inches high and 3 1/4 inches at the widest (9 cm and 8.5 cm). Then, pieces of green glass tile that has been previously cut with pliers are glued on.

14. Both sides of the tree are covered with the pieces. They are arranged in such way that there is space left for the garland. Notice how there are narrow spaces across the shape.

15. The sides are covered with green water-based paint, the same color as the grout.

16. It is filled with green-colored grout and cleaned. Then the decorations made with red pins are introduced. To hang this ornament, we use the same system we used for the reindeer, which will be explained later.

17. To make a cardholder in the shape of a crown, the procedure for the support is the same as explained before. The assembly method is different, however. First, the shape of the ornament is drawn on a tile following the outline of the pattern. Then the pieces of glass and glass tile are cut out.

18. Later, following the composition created as a guide, the pieces are glued onto the expanded polystyrene with an appropriate adhesive. It is left to dry for 24 hours.

19. It is sealed with white grout and left to dry for 30 minutes, then cleaned. The sides of the crown are painted with silver water-based paint.

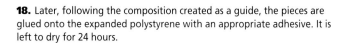

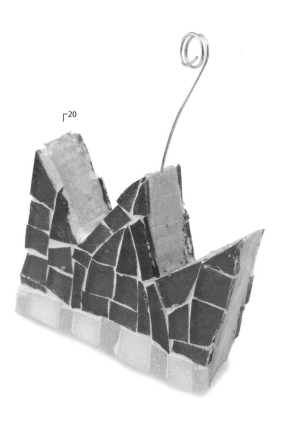

20. A 2 3/4-inch- (7-cm)-long piece of wire (twisted as shown in the picture) is inserted in the upper part of the ornament leaving 1 3/4 inches (4.5 cm) extended.

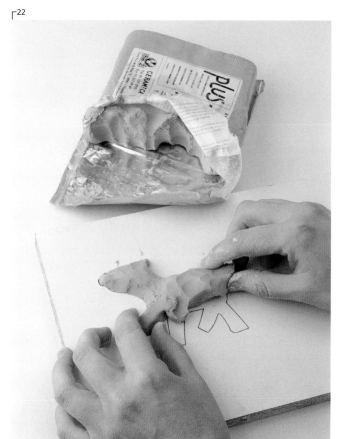

21. The 2 3/4-inch-high and 3 3/4-inch-wide (7-cm and 9.5-cm) reindeer is made of modeling clay and glass tile. It is very helpful to have a model as a guide on the work table at all times. To this end, the outline of the pattern is marked on the surface using a permanent marker with a heavy tip.

22. The top part of the ornament is modeled with the clay, following the drawing of the pattern.

23. The top and the sides are worked with a wooden spatula until a flat surface is achieved.

24. A hole is made with a piece of wire in the area where the antlers (made of wire) of the reindeer will be located when the mosaic is finished.

25. The glass tiles are cut with the pliers to the desired size, and the pieces inserted into the modeling clay.

26. It is left to dry and removed from the support or work surface. The manufacturer of the clay will indicate the drying time on the package, although it also depends on atmospheric conditions.

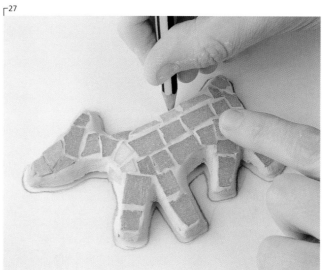

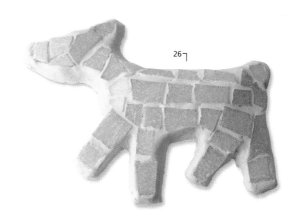

27. To make the second part of the figure, the opposite or the mirror image of the finished ornament is needed. The ornament is placed on a piece of paper and the outline is drawn with a pencil.

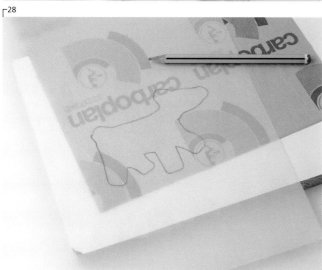

28. A piece of tracing paper is placed over the drawing. The pencil-drawn silhouette is traced, then it is turned over. The result is the mirror image of the figure. Finally, the line is redrawn with a permanent marker.

29. The second piece is made following the same procedure. Both parts of the ornament are identical and fit perfectly.

30. Adhesive cement, spread evenly on the reverse side of one of the pieces, is used to glue both together. Then the other piece is placed over the one with the glue and carefully aligned.

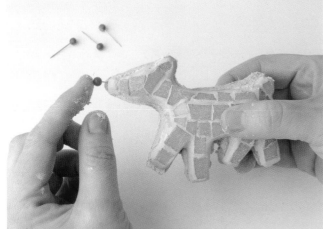

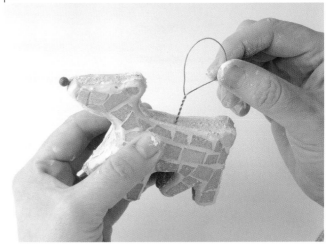

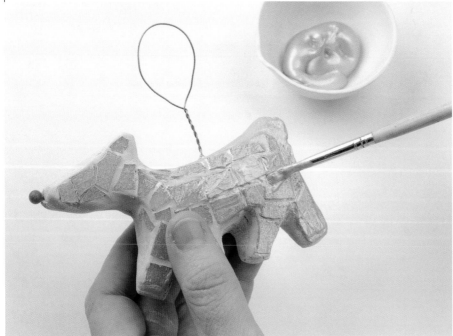

31. A red pin is inserted between both pieces to create the reindeer's nose.

32. A piece of wire is used to make the hook to hang the ornament. The wire is twisted to create a straight section at one end and a large loop at the other, then it is inserted in the center of the reindeer's back. The plaster is left to dry.

33. The joints and the grout between the pieces are painted with silver acrylic paint. It is left to dry. The excess paint on the pieces is removed by wiping it off with a paper towel.

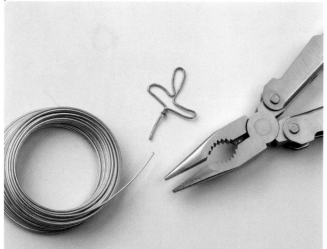

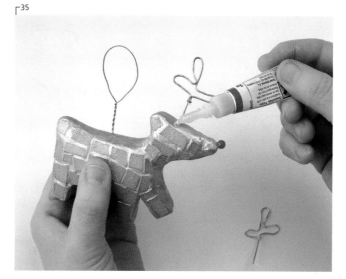

34. The 1 3/8-inch- (3.5-cm)-long reindeer antlers are made with wire of the same color as the loop, but thicker, using pliers.

35. A small drop of glue is placed inside the hole, then the antlers are inserted. They are held in place by hand for a few minutes until they seem securely attached. Another drop of glue is placed around the entry area to make it stronger. It is put aside for a minimum of 24 hours before hanging the ornament.

36. The finished ornaments.

Paving Blocks

The mosaic paving block is one of the best-known aspects of this art and the most commonly used throughout history. Mosaic allows the creation of resistant floor motifs of great esthetic value, whether they are displayed by themselves or integrated into the existing surface. The only limitation depends on the technical characteristics of the tile pieces themselves, that is, how resistant and durable they are in heavy traffic areas. This project shows how to make a mosaic paving block using the indirect method, meaning that the piece will be integrated into the existing floor in the interior of a house. The method presented here can be used either for indoors or outdoors, so it is the same for creating any type of mosaic paving block.

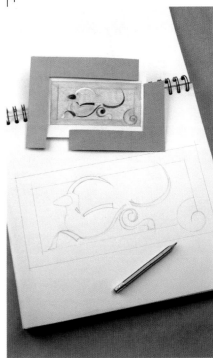

1. A color drawing is made of a figure or motif that will be integrated into a background that has brown tones. The 5 x 10-inch (13 x 26-cm) life-sized model is transferred onto paper.

2. Stoneware and glass tiles that complement the setting are used to create this mosaic.

3. To transfer the motif onto the temporary wrapping paper support, a pencil copy is traced on a piece of paper.

4. Tracing paper is placed on a piece of wrapping paper, which will be a little bit larger than the mosaic itself. The paper with the motif will be placed with the drawing side face down over the tracing paper. The different sheets are centered and secured with masking tape, and the design is traced.

5. The result is the mirror image of the motif on the temporary support. To make the mosaic, the tiles (cut to the desired size) are glued to the pattern.

6. The tile fragments are glued with the upper part face down (the one that will be visible when the mosaic is finished) in contact with the support. The main motif, the imaginary animal, is completed.

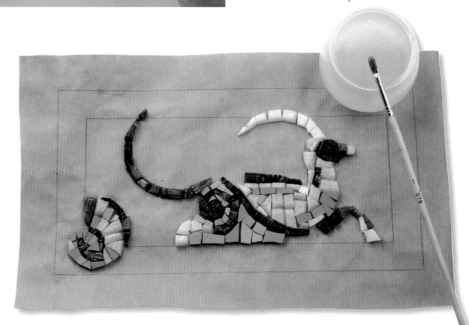

7. Now, the side motif, the seashell, is created.

8. The border that frames the composition is made with glass tiles of various blue tones, leaving a small separation between them.

9. The pieces that form the background (of different gray and ocher tones) are arranged in a wavy configuration following the lines of the mosaic's main motif. The line drawing on the paper will serve as a guide during this procedure.

10. The tiles that form the background are cut to the desired size, and glued, following the guidelines of the drawing.

11. The finished mosaic on the temporary support, ready to be placed on the floor of the house.

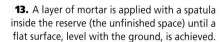

12. The mortar is prepared; in this case, it is adhesive floor cement.

13. A layer of mortar is applied with a spatula inside the reserve (the unfinished space) until a flat surface, level with the ground, is achieved.

14. The mosaic is dropped into the designated space with the tiles in direct contact with the mortar and the motif facing any direction chosen. It is important not to apply excessive pressure. To level the surface, a piece of wood is placed over the mosaic and tapped with a hammer until the decorative piece is set into the floor.

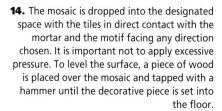

15

15. The paper is dampened with water and removed by pulling it gently to prevent the tiles from moving. Sometimes, a piece may come off when the mosaic is turned over to place it on top of the mortar. This can be fixed by replacing the pieces after the paper has been removed. In this case, since the adhesive cement material is between the joints, there is no need to grout the mosaic.

16. View of the decorative motif after the mural has dried, as part of the floor in the house.

16

Candleholder

One of the many possibilities offered by mosaic is the embellishment of surfaces that were constructed with common materials of little or no significant esthetic value. The layer of mosaic adds a new look and functionality to the object. This art is an excellent way of refurbishing and recycling objects because it can restore any element or surface. In this project, mosaic is used to decorate a recycled construction material (a small cement utility cover), which has been given a new use: an outdoor holder for candles. Some of the other materials used are also recycled, like the three saucers that will become the bases for the candles. The glass pieces scattered throughout the holder's base reflect the light, creating interesting effects. This mosaic is created using the direct system. The pieces are sealed with adhesive cement to simplify the process.

1. To create this candleholder we begin with a 17-inch (44-cm) outside diameter cement cover. White, gray, and light ocher color tiles are used, as well as a mirror and three blue ceramic plates.

2. The plates are placed inside the cement lid according to the arrangement desired. The outlines are drawn on the support with a pencil. The plates are fragmented using a hammer and pliers and the pieces arranged in the marked areas.

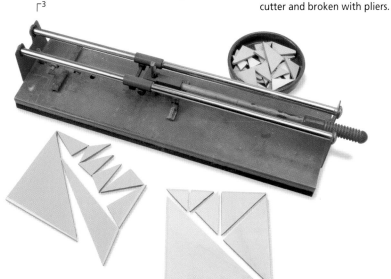

3. The tiles are cut in triangular sections with the tile cutter. Some of the triangles will be equilateral and others will have uneven sides.

4. The mirror is also cut in triangular sections of different sizes. A scoring line is made with the tile cutter or with a glass cutter and broken with pliers.

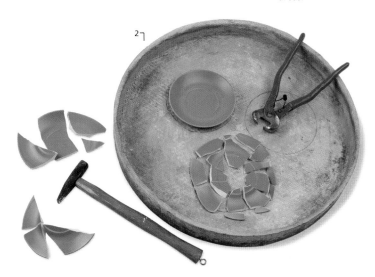

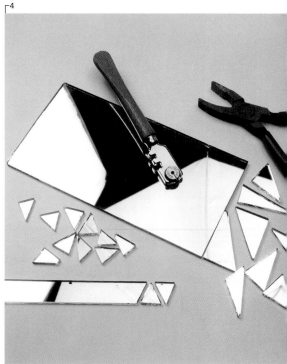

5. The mosaic is assembled by gluing the pieces with adhesive cement. First, one of the bases for the candle (the pieces of the saucer) is glued, followed by the background pieces that surround it, alternating triangular mirror fragments with different-colored tiles.

6. At the same time that the pieces are being glued, they are grouted with adhesive cement. This is done up to the inside edge of the lid.

5

6

7

7. The inside of the lid is covered with triangular pieces (mirrors and tiles) cut to the desired size but smaller than the previous ones.

8

8. The top edge is covered with fragmented or rectangular light ocher tiles. The adhesive cement is left to dry for a minimum of 24 hours, then the outside of the candleholder is painted with exterior white paint.

9. Outdoor candleholder used to decorate the garden.

Or as an indoor centerpiece or candleholder.

Wall Panel

The following project shows how to make a decorative piece, a wall panel, which will become part of the decor of a bedroom. To create the mosaic with the direct technique, some of the materials used, such as slate, are natural, and others, such as glass, ceramic tiles, and glass tiles are manufactured. They are attached to a medium density fiberboard (MDF) with mortar. The board will require some preliminary preparation to prevent it from warping, which could cause some pieces, even large sections of the work, to fall off. The painting is created from a very detailed design, which is transferred to the support using grid paper. In the step-by-step section we will demonstrate how to transfer any design to any surface, no matter how big it is, using the grid-paper method, adapting it to any creative process.

1. A design of the mosaic wall hanging that you wish to make is created. The 4.5 x 9.5-inch (12 x 24-cm) color drawing serves as a guide for transferring the motif to the support and also during the entire assembly process.

2. Next, a grid is made over the design. A sheet of tracing paper is placed over the graph paper and the grid is copied by drawing lines 3/4 inch (2 cm) apart.

3. Then the tracing paper is placed over the project, securing it at the corners with masking tape.

4. The support is a 48 x 24-inch (120 x 60-cm), 3/4-inch (2-cm)-thick fiberboard panel. Two coats of sealant are applied to make it waterproof and to prevent it from warping due to the effect of the mortar. The sealant is applied to the front and to the sides, letting it dry after each coat.

5. When the surface is dry, a grid is made by drawing lines 4 inches (10 cm) apart. A T-square is used to make perfectly straight parallel lines with respect to the support's sides.

6. The design is transferred to the support with a pencil, using the grid that we have made of the model as a reference.

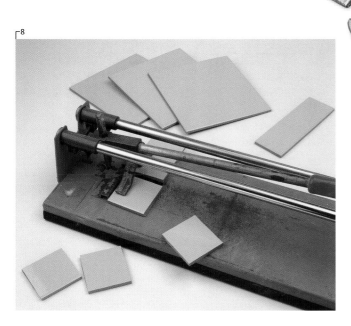

7. The materials for the mosaic are chosen according to the tones of the drawing and the dimensions of the piece. For this particular piece we have used glazed ceramic tiles, glass tiles, slate, and glass.

8. The assembly of the mosaic begins by creating the outside border. This is done by cutting the light ocher tiles in small 2 x 2-inch (5 x 5-cm) squares.

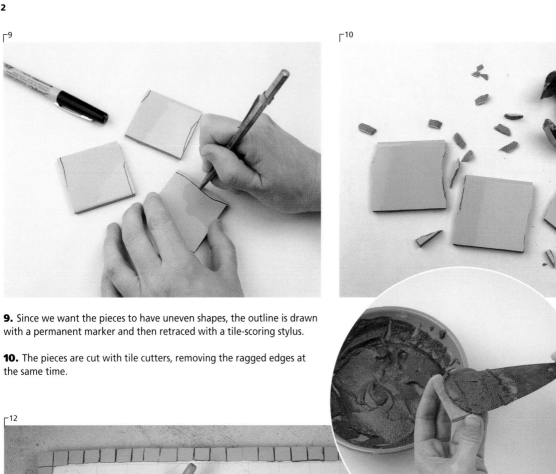

9. Since we want the pieces to have uneven shapes, the outline is drawn with a permanent marker and then retraced with a tile-scoring stylus.

10. The pieces are cut with tile cutters, removing the ragged edges at the same time.

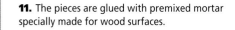

11. The pieces are glued with premixed mortar specially made for wood surfaces.

12. The pieces that form the sides and upper part of the border are attached first. Then the ceramic and glass tile pieces (previously cut) that form the main motif follow, proceeding in order from bottom to top.

13. All the pieces are glued in phases, leaving the spaces designated for the slate empty, then the portion of the bottom border is assembled.

14. The mosaic with all the pieces except the slate.

15. The slate is cut with a cold chisel or with a hammer and chisel. A block of expanded polystyrene is used as support for the stone, which will be split with a chisel.

16. Slate is a heavier material than tile and glass and requires a two-part adhesive to attach it to the wood.

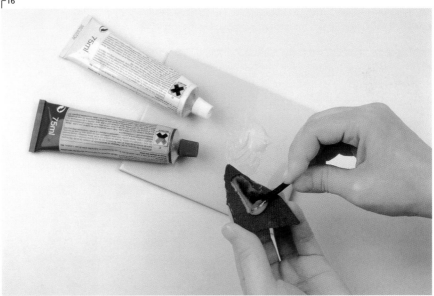

17. It is left to dry for a minimum of 24 hours.

18. Strips of wood are attached to the sides to form a frame, which is protected with masking tape before grouting begins.

19. The same mortar is used to seal the mosaic. It is applied with a plastic scraper, using enough pressure to make sure that the mortar penetrates all the joints.

20. It is left to dry for a minimum of 30 minutes, after which time the mortar left on the tiles is wiped off with a wet rag.

21. To clean the edges, a synthetic brush (toothbrush) is used.

22. The mosaic is left to dry for 24 hours. After that time, the masking tape that protects the frame is removed.

23. To enhance the color of the slate, a coat of colorless wax is applied over it. It is left to dry for one hour and then polished with a cotton rag.

24. The mosaic is hung the same as a painting.

23

22
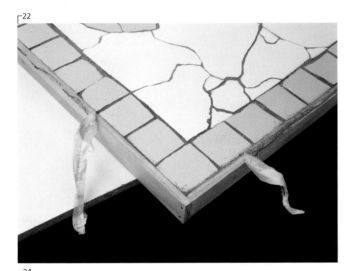

24

Table

A single mosaic project can combine several techniques. The pieces made with different styles afford the opportunity to combine various arrangements that produce very creative solutions. This project shows how to make an outdoor tabletop, which is decorated with a central motif using the indirect technique, surrounded by a background applied with the direct technique. Once the central mosaic piece is designed on a paper support, the board is created step by step. The same technique used to make floor mosaics is applied, in this case, because an outdoor table has to be strong and sturdy. A mortar mold is made inside a metal ring, which encases and defines the surface. A steel mesh is added to make a strong structure, then the background is created, and finally the central decorative design is added using the indirect construction method.

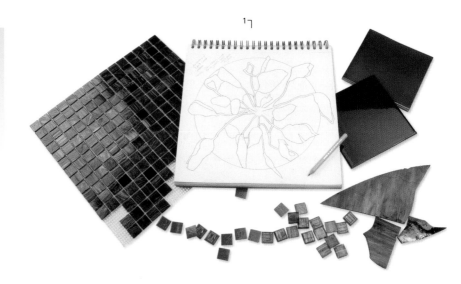

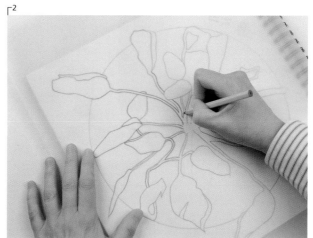

1. The 10-inch (25.5-cm)-diameter design with floral and garden motifs, which will be placed in the center of the board, is drawn on paper. Glass tile of various colors and glass will be used, and for the background (the area that surrounds the design) green tiles will be used.

2. A pencil drawing of the design is made on a piece of paper.

3. The motif is transferred to the temporary support. A sheet of tracing paper is placed over the wrapping paper (a little larger than the mosaic), with the surface containing the pencil drawing face down, and the design is copied.

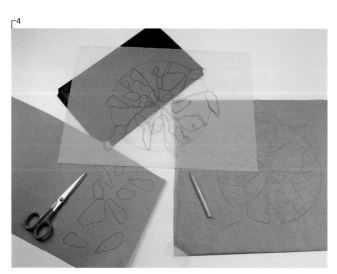

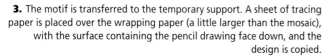

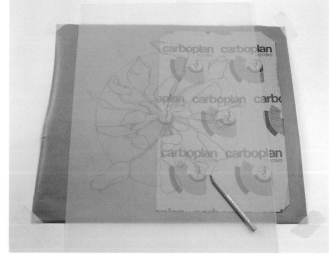

4. The motif transferred onto the temporary support is the mirror (inverted) image of the original. Next, templates of the glass pieces are made by tracing the outlines on cardboard.

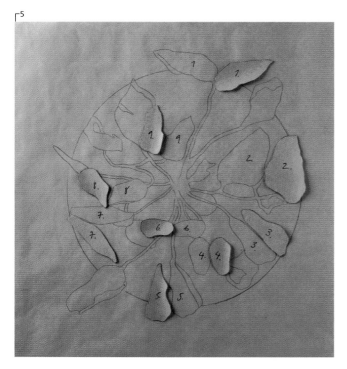

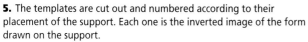

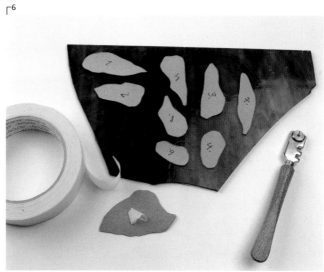

5. The templates are cut out and numbered according to their placement of the support. Each one is the inverted image of the form drawn on the support.

6. They are secured with masking tape to the glass (which will be visible once the mosaic is finished) that will be in contact with the support, to prevent them from moving.

7. The glass is cut a size slightly larger than the pattern.

8. Following the pattern's outline, the scoring line is marked with the cutter in steps, then the pieces are separated with pliers.

9. The edges are filed with the dressing stone until the desired profile is achieved.

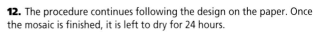

10. The pieces are glued to the support with methylcellulose glue. First, some of the glass pieces are attached.

11. The work progresses in an organized manner; the glass tiles are attached next. They are glued with their tops in contact with the support.

12. The procedure continues following the design on the paper. Once the mosaic is finished, it is left to dry for 24 hours.

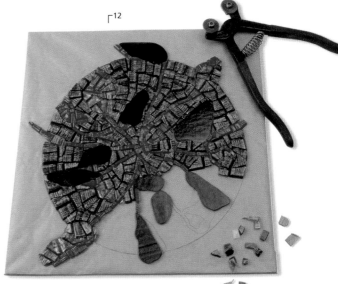

13. The excess wrapping paper is trimmed off and a pattern of the form is made. The mosaic is placed on a piece of paper and a pencil outline is made, which is then cut out.

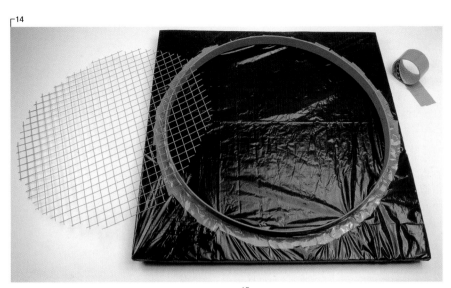

14. To make the top, a 1- to 1 1/2-inch (3-cm)-high and 21-inch (54-cm)-diameter metal ring, which has been previously painted, is placed over a flat waterproof surface (in this case, a board covered with plastic). The support is secured on the outside with plastic tape to form a mold for the mortar.

15. The mortar is poured inside the metal ring to form a 3/4-inch (19-mm)-thick layer, which is leveled out with a scraper.

16. A screen is placed on top of the mortar and covered with a layer similar to the previous one. This layer is smoothed out as well. The work surface is tapped several times to eliminate the bubbles from the mortar. Then the surface is covered with a piece of plastic and left to rest for three days.

17. The plastic is removed and the board is separated from the support. The pattern with the main motif is placed in the center of the board and the outline is drawn with a pencil.

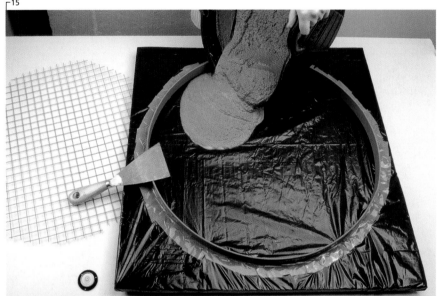

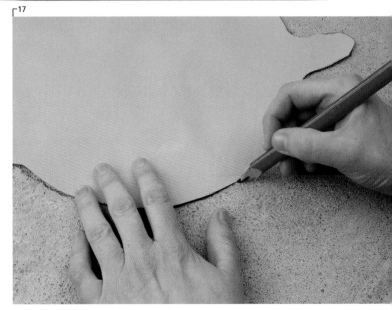

18. The outer area of the ring is covered with ceramic tile pieces alternating several green tones using the direct method.

19. As the work progresses the pieces are leveled with respect to each other and to the ring, tapping gently with a mallet on a piece of wood. It is left to dry.

20. The central area (where the motif will be placed using the indirect method) is dampened by spraying a small amount of water, then the mortar is applied.

21. The area is covered with a smooth and even layer of mortar, a little below the level of the surrounding tiles. The change in level is needed so the central mosaic, once inserted, is even with the tiles to the sides, in other words, the level of the mortar will be defined by the thickness of the pieces that form the motif.

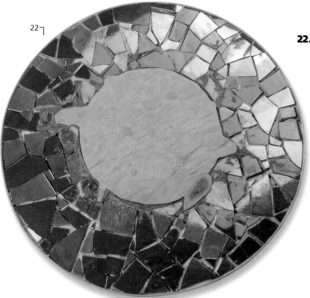

22⌐

22. The mosaic is placed in the center without applying too much pressure.

⌐23

23. It is leveled by tapping with a mallet on a larger board placed over the motif. The tapping is repeated until the surface is flat and leveled with the rest of the board.

24. The paper is dampened with water and removed by pulling gently.

⌐24

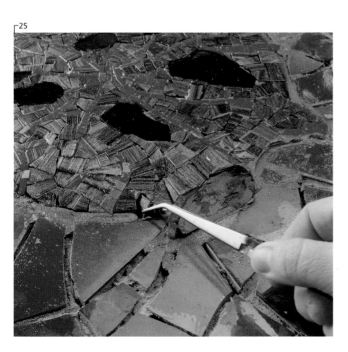
⌐25

25. It is possible that while removing the paper some pieces will move out of place. This is corrected by adjusting the pieces with tweezers.

26. The excess mortar lodged in the joints is removed with a thin pick, then it is left to dry for at least 24 hours.

27. Finally, the mosaic is filled with black grout and left to dry for 30 minutes, then it is wiped with a piece of paper towel. The metal ring is painted with a black metal paint for exterior use and the board is mounted on the stand.

28. The finished table in its setting outdoors.

Detail Integrated in a Tile Wall

One of the most spectacular applications of mosaic is the integrating of decorative details in a tiled floor or wall. This decorative solution, although time-consuming, is not difficult. Its most complicated procedure rests in the planning of the steps during the process. Therefore, to integrate the mosaic it is necessary to leave an empty space, in other words, an area without tiles where the mosaic will later be incorporated and surrounded by tiles similar to those already there.

Here, we show the process for integrating a motif into a tiled bathroom wall. A 36 × 12-inch (96 × 32-cm) empty space was left within a 2 × 2-inch (5 × 5-cm) tile frame when the wall was tiled, that is, an empty space of 18 × 6 tiles. The mosaic will be made of glass tiles, glass, stoneware, and enamel tiles using the double indirect method, and because of its dimensions will be placed on the wall in two stages. The arrangement on the final support shown here can be applied to any other mosaic of large dimensions.

1. In this case, the motif is designed based on a natural element, a string of peppers purchased in the market. A pencil sketch is made first, then it is redrawn with ink.

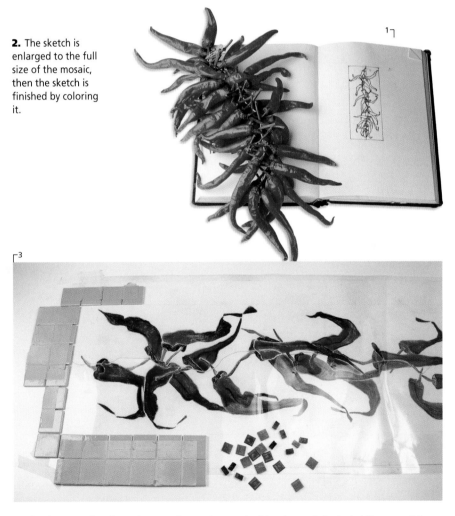

2. The sketch is enlarged to the full size of the mosaic, then the sketch is finished by coloring it.

3. The design is placed on a large surface and covered with a sheet of plastic, holding everything in place with masking tape. To arrange the motif on the wall with respect to the existing tile and to establish the frame that will surround the mosaic itself, it is necessary to use the original tiles as a guide. The 2 x 2-inch (5 x 5-cm) tiles are placed around the sketch, keeping in mind the 1/10-inch (3-mm) space for the joints.

4. The work is carried out in order. First, the outside tiles are glued with methylcellulose glue, followed by those that will be in contact with the mosaic. They are arranged so that they will appear in the finished mosaic, with the surface facing up. The outside frame and the spacing of the joints are respected at all times.

5. The mosaic is arranged by area. The color design serves as a guide as far as color and as a pattern for the shapes. The pieces are cut and attached with glue.

6. The shape of the tile is marked with permanent marker, then it is cut following the line. This way the tile fits perfectly around the mosaic.

7. The tiles are glued and arranged in an organized way, by area, until the work is finished.

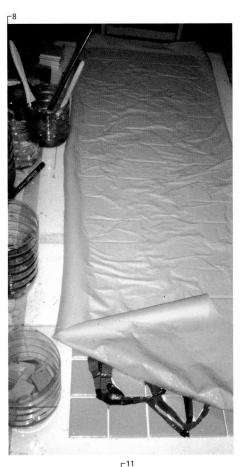

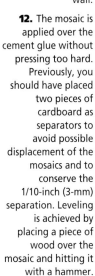

8. Wrapping paper (somewhat larger than the work) is prepared and glue is applied to one of its sides. The paper is centered on the design with the glued side touching the mosaic, and it is gently pressed over it. It is left to dry.

9. The mosaic with the paper and the plastic is placed between two pieces of wood or any other hard material large enough to hold the work. Then it is turned over and the plastic sheet is removed.

10. Given the dimensions of this mosaic, it is attached to the wall in two stages. The mosaic is separated into two parts, cutting the temporary support along the outlines of the pieces and the tiles. This way the mosaic will be in two pieces, one of them approximately two-thirds (the lower part) and the other one-third (the top part). The excess paper is trimmed off.

11. First, you affix the lower part, the largest piece of the mosaic. You apply a layer of cement glue on the area that you want to cover, until you have a flat surface which is level with the rest of the wall.

12. The mosaic is applied over the cement glue without pressing too hard. Previously, you should have placed two pieces of cardboard as separators to avoid possible displacement of the mosaics and to conserve the 1/10-inch (3-mm) separation. Leveling is achieved by placing a piece of wood over the mosaic and hitting it with a hammer.

13. The operation is repeated by fitting the top portion with the bottom one.

14. The wrapping paper is dampened with water and removed by gently pulling. To prevent tiles from moving or becoming displaced, the paper is removed diagonally.

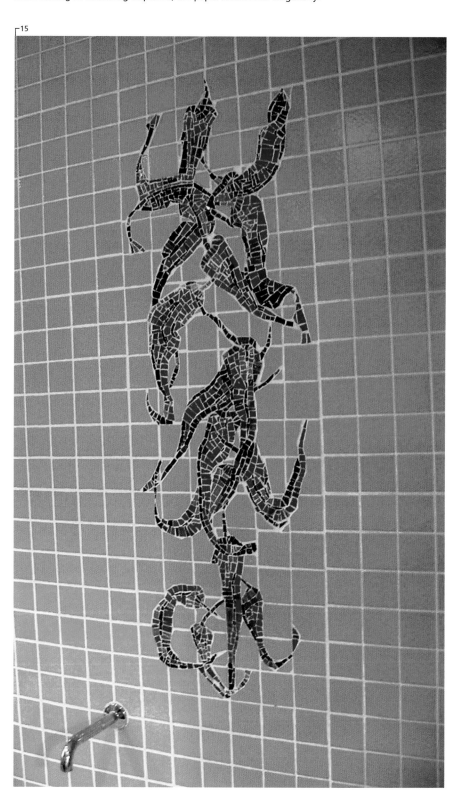

15. The excess adhesive cement is eliminated from the surface of the tiles, pieces, and joints. The piece is sealed with the same grout used for the rest of the wall. Finally, the surface is cleaned. The result is a decorative piece that fits perfectly into the tiled wall.

Border

In this project, the design of the previous motif is adapted, reinterpreting it to decorate another room in the same house. This shows the many different possibilities offered by a single design. Therefore, the shapes of the decorative details form the basis to create three new designs for a border that will decorate a kitchen wall in a triptych fashion.

As with the previous project, three empty spaces are left with the tiled surface. In the close to 11-feet (330-cm)-long wall, three areas 3 feet by 6 inches (15 × 90 cm) long are left empty—in other words, three empty spaces of six tiles each separated by two tiles and with two additional tiles at each end. The mosaic is created with the double indirect method. Other variations from the previous project are the materials and the color.

1. The existing design from the previous project is taken as a starting point. The new design is the result of a different interpretation of the old one, which has been broken down into several motifs. Parts of the original forms are traced on paper with a pencil according to the size that each part will be on the border. The result is three different copies representing the two halves and the middle part of the original respectively.

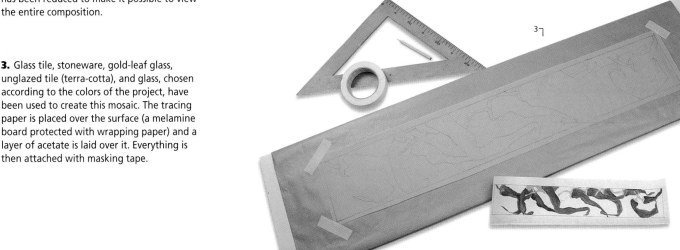

2. The patterns are photocopied and colored to complete the design of the border. The size has been reduced to make it possible to view the entire composition.

3. Glass tile, stoneware, gold-leaf glass, unglazed tile (terra-cotta), and glass, chosen according to the colors of the project, have been used to create this mosaic. The tracing paper is placed over the surface (a melamine board protected with wrapping paper) and a layer of acetate is laid over it. Everything is then attached with masking tape.

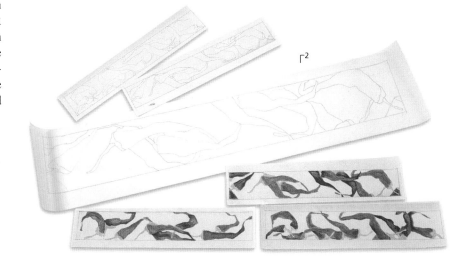

4. The pieces (previously cut) that form the motif, the peppers, are glued with methylcellulose adhesive, following the design as reference.

5. The background is created with fragments of terra-cotta tiles.

6. The pieces for the background are glued as well with the tops facing up. The pieces are adjusted with the pliers as needed so they fit perfectly in the composition.

7. The work continues by completing the mosaic by area. The background, as well as the motif, are worked together.

8. A view of one of the sections of the finished border. The other two parts are created following the same procedure.

9. Glue is applied to one side of a piece of wrapping paper that is somewhat larger in size than the work, and it is placed over the mosaic. This mosaic is a special case because the various pieces that form the design have different thicknesses, creating different levels. To make sure that the pieces stay in place, a layer of glue is applied to the wrapping paper. It is left to dry for 24 hours.

10. To remove the plastic sheet from the mosaic, a knife is run underneath as the plastic is being removed.

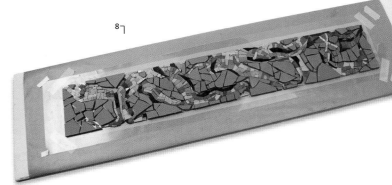
8⌐

⌐9

⌐10

⌐11

11. If any piece becomes dislodged, it is put back into place and glued.

12. A thin and even layer of adhesive cement is applied to the reserved area. The adhesive cement is marked with a notched trowel to make the mosaic adhere better. Another layer is applied to the backside of the mosaic, completely filling in the uneven areas.

13. The mosaic is placed over the layer of adhesive cement without applying too much pressure. Each part of the border is set according to the desired arrangement. They are then leveled by placing a piece of wood over the mosaic and tapping it with a hammer, then the paper is dampened and lifted by pulling gently.

14. This is the time to correct small problems by realigning the pieces with a knife or a spatula, or replacing them. If some pieces have been lost, new ones can be added.

15. The mosaic is grouted with adhesive cement. A generous amount is applied with a plastic scraper, making sure that it penetrates into the joints between the pieces. Before this layer dries completely, the excess adhesive cement is removed with a dampened sponge. It is left to dry for 24 hours.

16. View of the border that decorates the kitchen.

Another option for the finish would have been to seal the background with a grout of the same color as the tile, leaving the motifs with the white grout.

Glossary

Andamenti
An Italian term that designates the placement of the pieces of the mosaic.

Backsplash
A piece that is attached to the wall just above a sink to protect the surface from splashes.

Chiaroscuro
Effects resulting from the contrasts of light and shadow on the surface of a work. In mosaics, chiaroscuro is an effect of illumination of the surface or pieces of a volume.

Cold Chisel
This is a Metal tool that is used for cutting stonelike materials. It has a triangular section, with a sharp edge at the top and a cylindrical base. The latter is inserted into a tree stump with a wooden box or tray that acts as a base. The cut is made by striking the piece supported on the sharp edge with a hammer.

Contrast
Counterpoint or opposition of the notable differences between two elements. In mosaic, contrasts are defined by color, placement, shape, and size of the pieces or their different materials, for example.

Curing
Refers to the hardening of materials such as lime, plaster, and mortar as they dry, which allows a work done using them to be attached and worked in a consistent manner.

Direct Placement
Technique consisting of directly attaching the pieces to the permanent support with adhesive or mortar.

Double Indirect Placement
Technique in which provisional supports are used, appropriate for mosaics made with pieces whose front is different from the back. They are first assembled on a provisional support, placing the pieces or tiles exactly the way they are to look when finished. Next, the second support is attached to the top surface of the mosaic, the work is turned over, and the first support is removed. Then the mosaic is attached to the final support following the indirect system.

Emblemata
Portable mosaics of the Roman Era created on rigid supports, such as marble or ceramic plaques. When finished they were treated like paintings or they were inserted as a central element into floors that were previously covered in mosaic work.

Enamel Tiles
Tiles made of opaque glass paste. These tiles, approximately 5/16 × 3/16 inches (1.5 × 1 cm) are hand-cut from the larger glass pieces, causing them to have discontinuous and irregular surfaces.

Fragmenting (pique assiette)
Breaking up the ceramic by striking the unglazed side with a hammer to create irregular pieces of different sizes that fit together. Fragmenting will allow any surface to be covered, no matter how complicated, with ceramic mosaic.

Frame
Structure made with pieces of wood (slats and boards) or metal to support and give form to the mortar while it sets up.

Glass Cutter
Tool consisting of a handle with a cutting wheel at one end that cuts as it turns. It is used to score lines in glass. It is also called a roulette.

Grout
The paste or mortar used to fill the joints between the pieces of a mosaic.

Indirect Placement
Technique in which the mosaic is made, in the first stage, on a provisional support, adhering the pieces to it upside down. Then it is attached to the final support and the provisional support is removed. This method is used when the front and back of the pieces are the same.

Indirect Placement for Pavers
Technique or placement system in which the mosaic is made following the indirect technique on a temporary support. It is placed inside a mold, then mortar is poured into it. When the mortar has set, the frame is disassembled and the provisional support removed.

Joint

The open space left between two pieces or tiles. The joints are filled with grout or mortar after assembling the mosaic, although on occasion they can be left unfilled.

Lithostrate

Pavement made by embedding stones directly into mortar on the floor or ground.

Mold

A frame that can be disassembled that holds concrete or cement while it cures.

Mortar

The mixture used by masons and mosaic artists for attaching pieces to the final support. It is made by mixing different components (cement with sand and lime in some cases) in various proportions in water or by adding water to a premixed commercial product.

Opus

Latin term meaning *work, to work,* or *labor.* Today it is used as a generic term to refer to the work or system of placing the blocks and mosaics. There is also *opus spicatum* (placement in the form of a thorn or splinter), *opus sectile* (placing stone pieces in geometric forms), *opus vermiculatum* (following the outlines of the motif), *opus quadratum* (placing square or rectangular pieces in rows), among others.

Paramento

Either of the two sides of a wall.

Piece

Refers to each part that makes up a mosaic, particularly the ones that are not shaped like tiles.

Placement

Refers to the order and system of assembling the pieces of a mosaic.

Release Agent

Substance that is put on a surface so that no other material can become permanently adhered to it. It is applied to the surface as a thin film, to protect it and separate it so that other materials, such as mortar, will not stick to it.

Reserve

This is an area on the surface of a piece of glass that is protected by one of several methods from the action of an acid cream. It is also the area of a wall that is left open where a mosaic is to be located.

Rhythm

A combination using a succession or a specific pattern of pieces in a mosaic. The rhythm in a work can be created by the forms and size of the pieces, their placement, the tones and colors, etc.

Roulette

(See glass cutter.)

Scored Line

The line made by a glass cutter on the surface of the glass to mark where the material will fracture when force is applied.

Tile Cutter

Tool consisting of a small disk of hardened steel that scores a cutting line, attached to a handle that moves between two guides. It is used for cutting wall and floor tile, as well as very thick pieces of glass.

Tile Marking Stylus

Instrument shaped like a pencil that has a sharp point used for scoring tiles, pliers are then used to break them along the scored line.

To Laminate

Refers to adhering one piece of glass to another, sometimes with some material placed in between them.

To Level

To even the surface of a mosaic, either the pieces that may be different heights, or in respect to the surfaces around it.

Sealer

Commercial liquid used to cover porous surfaces like that of wood. It is not very oily and it dries fast to make a hard, waterproof surface.

Sinopia

Preparatory drawing made on the wall when painting frescoes. It is usually red in color, and it serves as a sort of guide or pattern for the daily work.

Smalti

Italian name for enamel tiles. (See enamels.)

Support

Surface to which the mosaic is attached. Supports are often provisional, which are used to hold the mosaic while it is being assembled, then they are removed when it is permanently installed.

Tessera

From the word *tesella* which in Latin means *cube.* Refers to all the pieces that form a mosaic, and in particular, those that have a square or rectangular shape.

Texture

Characteristic surface structure of a material or an element that can be seen and especially appreciated by touch.

Trencadís

Original Catalan word for fragmenting, an approach that was originally the idea of and used by Catalan architects during the Modernist Period for creating mosaics integrated with the architecture.

ACKNOWLEDGMENTS

The authors would like to thank:

Editorial Parramón, especially María Fernanda Canal, for trusting us with this project. Also Joan Soto and the entire team at Nos & Soto for their dedication, kindness, and help; José Antonio Ares for his great kindness; María Rosa Dalmau, Mary Ledwith, and Annie Michie for their help and assistance with our project; Mark for his help, patience, and understanding, and Helen.

These companies for their generous collaboration:

Arena professional
Fusina, 11
08003 Barcelona
www.arenaprofesional.com
info@arenaprofesional.com

La Crafteria
Materiales para bellaas artes
Talleres infantiles y adultos
Pl. Surtidor, 15
08004 Barcelona
www.crafteria.eresmas.net

Marbres Bardou
Avda. Paral.lel, 112
08015 Barcelona

As well as the collaborating artists:

Ellen Darlene Stern
Mosaic Artist
Michigan
USA www.americanmosaics.com

Livia Garreta
Taller de mosaico Livia Garret y Marta Clua
Pere Serafi, 39
08012 Barcelona
www.liviagarreta.com

Damian Morrison
Fusina, 11
08003 Barcelona

Sebastiá Vilarasau
Interiorista. Diseñador
Pádua, 14, ático 1ª
08023 Barcelona
DISS.vilarasau@teleline.es

La Ventana Indiscreta
Magalhäes, 36, bajos
08004 Barcelona
www.phillipabeveridge.com

MOSAICS

Original title of the book in Spanish: *Mosaico*
©Copyright 2004 by PARRAMON EDICIONES, S.A.,—World Rights
Published in 2004 by Parramon Ediciones, S.A., Barcelona, Spain.

Translated from the Spanish by Michael Brunelle and Beatriz Cortabarria

All inquiries should be addressed to:
Barron's Educational Series, Inc.
250 Wireless Blvd.
Hauppauge, NY 11788
www.barronseduc.com

ISBN-13: 978-0-7641-3229-2
ISBN-10: 0-7641-3229-6

Library of Congress Catalog Card No.
2004115827

Text: Eva Pascual
Exercises: Philippa Beveridge with the cooperatiion of Verónica Winters for the project "Christmas Decorations"

Photography: Estudio Nos & Soto, Mark Waudby, Philippa Beveridge, A. Gautier

Printed in Spain
9 8 7 6 5 4 3 2 1